EMIGRANTS
FROM SCOTLAND
TO AMERICA

1774 — 1775

Copied from a Loose Bundle of Treasury Papers
in the Public Record Office
London, England

COMPILED AND INDEXED IN THE LONDON OFFICE OF
VIOLA ROOT CAMERON
GENEALOGIST

Baltimore
GENEALOGICAL PUBLISHING CO., INC.
1980

291491

Originally produced: London, 1930
Reprinted: Southern Book Company
Baltimore, 1959
Reissued: Genealogical Publishing Co., Inc.
Baltimore, 1965, 1976, 1980
Library of Congress Catalogue Card Number 61-40562
International Standard Book Number 0-8063-0066-3
Made in the United States of America

(P.R.O.) (T. 47/12)

Port Greenock.   List of Passengers from the 3rd of Feby. excle.

to the 10th of February 1774 inclusive.

Names	Former Residence.	Age.	Occupation	To what Port or Place Bound.	*On what Account and for what purpose they go.
John Drumond	Paisley	19	Weaver	New York	
Robert Stewart	do.	17	Labourer	do.	
Mary Bell	do.	23	Spinster	do.	
Hugh Dunsmuir	do.	40	Weaver	do.	
James Spence	do.	25	Cart Wright	do.	
John McFarlane	Glasgow	17	Hatter	do.	
James Horley	do.	20	Weaver	do.	
Adam Horley	do.	11	do.	do.	
William Fleming	do.	16	do.	do.	
Daniel Mair	do.	35	do.	do.	
Robert White	do.	16	do.	do.	
Alexander Baxter	do.	33	Butcher	do.	
Mary Howet	do.	25	Spinster	do.	
James Young	do.	23	Labourer	do.	
Thomas Smith	do.	17	Weaver	do.	
William Clark	do.	20	Shoemaker	do.	
William McNeil	Faisley	17	Weaver	do.	
James Knox	do.	21	do.	do.	
John Wallace	do.	25	do.	do.	
Angus Sewter	do.	16	Spinster(sic)	do.	
Lillias Campbell	do.	16	do.	do.	
Margaret Suster	do.	18	do.	do.	
Ann Cooper	Wick	21	do.	do.	
Nelly Dunmore	Paisley	26	do.	do.	
Cristian McNeil	do.	20	do.	do.	
Margaret McQueen	do.	18	do.	do.	
Angus McKenzie	do.	17	do.	do.	
Alexander Aitken	do.	17	Weaver	do.	
Ninian Calder	do.	18	do.	do.	
John Wardrobe	Glasgow	30	Taylor	do.	
John McLeod, Junr.	do.	14	do.	do.	
John McLeod, Senr.	do.	35	do.	do.	
Florence Munro	do.	20	Spinster	do.	
Archibald Scott	do.	26	Taylor	do.	
Joseph Wilson	do.	19	Puiterer	do.	
Robert Leitch	do.	28	Farmer	do.	
Joseph Paton	do.	29	do.	do.	
James Stater	do.	40	Chapman	do.	
Ann Honeybull	do.	33	Spinster	do.	

* For Poverty and to get Bread.

In the "Commerce." Duncan Ferguson Master for New York.

John Tanyhill	do.	19	Farmer	do.
Robert Tanyhill	do.	25	do.	do.
Hugh Robb	do.	39	Taylor	do.
Alexander Yuill	do.	27	Wright	do.
James McKennot	do.	28	Copper Smith	do.
Thomas McAllaster	do.	20	Shoemaker	do.
James Murdoch	do.	31	Gardener	do.
James Kerita	do.	27	Labourer	do.
John Beggar	Paisley	20	Taylor	do.
William Calder	do.	35	Weaver	do.
Angus Roder nis Wife	do.	31	Spinster (sic)	do.
James Calder his Child.	do.	17	Weaver	do.
Angus Calder do.	do.	15	Spinster	do.
Marget Calder do.	do.	12	do.	do.
Elizabeth Calder do.	do.	10	do.	do.
Robert Calder do.	do.	7		do.
William Paton	do.	32	Weaver	do.
Mary his Wife	do.	27	Spinster (sic)	do.
Janet Paton his Child	do.	15	do.	do.
Margaret his do.	do.	13	do.	do.
Cathrine do.	do.	10	do.	do.
William Murchie	do.	37	Weaver	do.
Agnes his Wife	do.	32	Spinster (sic)	do.
William Murchie	do.	16	Weaver	do.
James Murchie	do.	15	do.	do.
John Murchie	do.	13	do.	do.
Gavin Murchie	do.	11	do.	do.
Robert Muir	do.	30	do.	do.
Jane his Wife	do.	29	Spinster (sic)	do.
Margaret his Dau.	do.	14	do.	do.
Ann do.	do.	12	do.	do.
James his Son	do.	7		do.
James Cunningham	do.	42	Weaver	do.
Elizabeth his Wife	do.	40	Spinster	do.
do. his Dau.	do.	20	do.	do.
Cathrine do.	do.	18	do.	do.
Donald his Son	do.	16	Weaver	do.
James his do.	do.	14	do.	do.
William his do.	do.	12	do.	do.
Sarah his Dau.	do.	5		do.
Ronald McDonald	do.	31	Weaver	do.
Mary his Wife	do.	28		do.
Walter Dougal	do.	42	Weaver	do.
Susannah his Wife	do.	39		do.
William his Child	do.	18	Weaver	do.
Alexander his do.	do.	16	do.	do.
Hugh his do.	do.	14	do.	do.
Robert his do.	do.	12	do.	do.
Susanah do.	do.	7		do.
John Spence	do.	29	Weaver	do.
Margaret his Wife	do.	27	Spinster	do.
John Lang	do.	30	Weaver	do.
Margaret his Wife	do.	28	Spinster	do.

For Poverty and to get Bread.

In the "Commerce." Duncan Ferguson Master for New York.

John Connel	do.	39	Weaver	do.
Barbara his Wife	do.	37		do.
Robert his Child	do.	16	Weaver	do.
Margaret do.	do.	14		do.
Jean do.	do.	12	Spinster	do.
John do.	do.	10	Weaver	do.
James do.	do.	4		do.
James Robertson	do.	32	Weaver	do.
Jean his Wife	do.	27		do.
James his Child	do.	12	Weaver	do.
Robert do.	do.	10	do.	do.
Jean do.	do.	7		do.
John Crawford	do.	35	Weaver	do.
Margaret his Wife	do.	29	Spinster	do.
Lawrence his Child	do.	13	do.	do.
Margaret do.	do.	10	do.	do.
John his do.	do.	8		do.
William Scott junr.	do.	25	Weaver	do.
Margaret his Wife	do.	21	Spinster	do.
William Scott, senr.	do.	39	Weaver	do.
Margaret his Wife	do.	38	Spinster	do.
John his Son	do.	11	Weaver	do.
Margaret Robison	do.	28	Spinster	do.
James Buchan a Child	do.	10		do.
Jean Crawford	do.	27	Spinster	do.
John Orr her Son	do.	11		do.
William Templeton	do.	27	Weaver	do.
Margaret his Wife	do.	25	Spinster	do.
Charles Sewter	do.	31	Weaver	do.
Elizabeth his Wife	do.	30	Spinster	do.
James Thornton	do.	9		do.
James Sewter	do.	35	Weaver	do.
Jean his Wife	do.	31	Spinster	do.
Ann his Child	do.	10	do.	do.
Colin Gibson	do.	25	Taylor	do.
Jannet his Wife	do.	23		do.
Thomas McCrae	do.	27		do.
Elizabeth his Wife	do.	23	Spinster	do
Jennat Aggie	do.	35	do.	do.
Margaret Aggie	do.	36	do.	do.
Cathrine Aggie	do.	11		do.
Barbra Aggie	do.	9		do.
John Wilson	do.	32	Weaver	do.
William his Son	do.	10	do.	do.
James his Son	do.	8		do.
Andrew Paterson	Glasgow	30	Sawer	do.
Elizabeth his Wife	do.	25	Spinster	do.
John his Child	do.	7		do.
Joseph Shirar	Paisley	30	Weaver	do.
Janet his Wife	do.	27	Spinster	do.
Archibald his Child	do.	10		do.
John Burns	do.	35	Weaver	do.

For Poverty and to get Bread

In the "Commerce." Duncan Ferguson Master for New York.

4

Margaret his Wife	do.	31	Spinster	do.
Robert Connell	do.	38	Labourer	do.
Elizabeth his Wife	do.	32	Spinster	do.
Alexander Glen	do.	36	Weaver	do.
Ann his Wife	do.	33	Spinster	do.
Jenat Hogie	do.	14	do.	do.
Elizabeth Ferguson	do.	27	do.	do.
Ann Orr	do.	18	do.	do.
Mary Jamieson	do.	24	do.	do.
Agnes Barr	do.	22	do.	do.
Isabella Orr	do.	20	do.	do.
Eliza Baird	do.	20	do.	do.
Jean Smith	do.	17	do.	do.
Cathrine Stewart	do.	18	do.	do.
Janet Pader	do.	20	do.	do.
Jean Adam	do.	22	do.	do.
Margaret Gibson	do.	16	do.	do.
Cathrine Aggie	do.	15	do.	do.
Marrion Ralston	do.	18	do.	do.
Mary Steel	do.	17	do.	do.
Agnes Agnee	do.	19	do.	do.
Agnes Blackhall	do.	26	do.	do.
Jannet Boyce	do.	16	do.	do.
Henry Neil	do.	18	do.	do.
Sary Campbell	do.	15	do.	do.
Donal McDonald	do.	16	Weaver	do.
Hugh Cameron	do.	18	do.	do.
William Gibson	do.	19	do.	do.
John Hutchison	do.	20	Weaver	do.
Thomas Smellie	do.	17	do.	do.
Ninian Hercules	do.	24	do.	do.
Walter Dougall	do.	17	do.	do.
Hugh McLellan	do.	17	do.	do.
Robert Muir	do.	17	do.	do.
William Murchie jun.	do.	18	do.	do.
William Campbell	do.	16	do.	do.
James Wilson	do.	19	Labourer	do.
David Ingles	do.	21	Weaver	do.
James Sowster	do.	15	do.	do.
Archibald McNeil	do.	23	do.	do.
John Rarity	do.	22	do.	do.
James Emiry	do.	20	do.	do.
John McCullock	do.	21	do.	do.
George Wilson	do.	19	Labourer	do.
John Boog	do ..	15	Weaver	do.
John Sim	do.	16	do.	do.
Alexander Wilson	do.	16	do.	do.
John McFarlane	Glasgow	19	Rope Maker	do.
John Russell	Paisley	16	Weaver	do.
William Muir	do.	17	do.	do.
John Muir	do.	17	do.	do.
James Miller	do.	21	do.	do.

For Poverty and to get Bread.

In the "Commerce." Duncan Ferguson Master for New York.

John Strachan	do.	16	do.	do.
Archibald Murdoch	do.	17	do.	do.
William Wilson	do.	30	do.	do.
James Allieson	do.	16	do.	do.
William Neilson	do.	20	do.	do.
James Nairne	do.	19	Smith	do.
Daniel Rankin	do.	18	Labourer	do.
John Browester	do.	21	Weaver	do.
William Schaw	do.	20	Labourer	do.
Robert Aitken	do.	18	Nailer	do.
Margaret Broa	do.	24	Spinster	do.
William Miller	do.	23	Weaver	do.
Margaret Craig	do.	19	Spinster	do.
Jennet Renfrew	do.	17	do.	do.
Elizabeth Bath	do.	21	do.	do.
James Dougal	do.	19	Weaver	do.

For Poverty and to get Bread

In the "Commerce." Duncan Ferguson Master for New York.

(Signed) (JO. CLERK C. Collector
(ALEXr. CAMPBELL D. Comptr.
(JOHN DUNLOP T.S.

(T. 47/12)

Report of the Examination of the Emigrants
from the Counties of Caithness and Sutherland
on board the Ship Bachelor of Leith
bound to Wilmington in North Carolina.

WILLIAM GORDON. Saith that he is aged Sixty and upwards,
by Trade a Farmer, married, hath Six Children, who
Emigrate with him, with the Wives and Children of his
two sons John & Alexander Gordon. Resided last at
Wynmore in the Parish of Clyne in the County of
Sutherland, upon Lands belonging to William Baillie
of Rosehall. That having two Sons already settled
in Carolina, who wrote him encouraging him to come
there, and finding the Rents of Lands raised in so much,
that a Possession for which his Grandfather paid only
Eight Merks Scots he himself at last paid Sixty, he was
induced to emigrate for the greater benefit of his
Children being himself an old Man and lame so that it
was indifferent to him in what Country he died. That
his Circumstances were greatly reduced not only by the
rise of Rents but by the loss of Cattle, particularly
in the severe Winter 1771. That the lands on which he
lived have often changed Masters, and that the Rents
have been raised on every Change; And when Mr. Baillie

bought them they were farmed with the rest of his
purchase to one Tacksman at a very high Rent, who must
also have his profits out of them. All these things
concurring induced him to leave his own Country in hopes
that his Children would earn their Bread more comfortably
elsewhere. That one of his Sons is a Weaver and another
a Shoe Maker and he hopes they may get bread for themselves
and be a help to support him.

WILLIAM McKAY. Aged Thirty, by Trade a Farmer, Married,
hath three Children from Eight to two years Old, besides
one dead since he left his own Country, resided last
at . . . . . in the Parish of Farr in the County of
Strathnaver, upon the Estate of the Countess of Sutherland,
Intends to go to Wilmington in North Carolina, because
his Stock being small, Crops failing, and bread excessively
dear, and the price of Cattle low, he found he could not
have bread for his Family at home, and was encouraged
to emigrate by the Accounts received from his Countrymen
who had gone to America before him, assuring him that
he might procure a Comfortable Subsistence in that
Country. That the land he possessed was a Wadset
of the Family of Sutherland to Mr. Charles Gordon of
Skelpick, lying in the height of the Country of
Strathnaver, the Rents were not raised.

W^m. SUTHERLAND, Aged Forty, a Farmer, Married, hath five

Children from 19 to 9 years old, lived last at
(sic)
Strathalidale in the Parish of Rea, in the County of

Caithness, upon the Estate of the late Colonel McKay

of Bighorne, Intends to go to North Carolina; left

his own Country because the Rents were raised, as

Soldiers returning upon the peace with a little Money

had offered higher Rents, and larger Fines or Grassums,

besides the Services were oppressive in the highest

degree. That from his Farm which paid 60 Merks Scots,

he was obliged to find two Horses and two Servants

from the middle of July to the end of Harvest solely

at his own Expense, besides plowing, Cutting Turf,

making Middings, mixing Dung and leading it out in

Seed time, and beside cutting, winning, leading and

stacking 10 Fathoms of Peats yearly, all done without

so much as a bit of bread or a drink to his Servants.

JOHN CATANOCK, Aged Fifty Years, by Trade a Farmer, Married,

hath 4 Children from 19 to 7 Years old; resided last at
(sic)
Chabster in the Parish of Rae, in the County of Caithness,

upon the Estate of Mr. Alex^r. Nicolson Minister at

Thurso, Intends to go to Wilmington in North Carolina;

left his own Country because Crops failed, Bread became

dear, the Rents of his possession were raised from Two

to Five Pounds Sterling, besides his Pasture or Common

Grounds were taken up by placing new Tenants thereon, especially the grounds adjacent to his Farm, which were the only grounds on which his Cattle pastured. That this method of parking and placing Tenants on the Pasture Grounds rendered his Farm useless, his Cattle died for want of Grass, and his Corn Farm was unfit to support his Family, after paying the Extravagant Tack duty. That beside the rise of Rents and Scarcity of bread, the Landlord exacted arbitrary and oppressive Services, such as obliging the Declarant to labour up his ground, cart, win, lead and stack his Peats, Mow, win and lead his Hay, and cut his Corn and lead it in the Yard which took up above 30 or 40 days of his Servants and Horses each year, without the least Acknowledgment for it, and without Victuals, save the men that mowed the Hay who got their Dinner only. That he was induced to Emigrate by Advices received from his Friends in America, that Provisions are extremely plenty & cheap, and the price of labour very high, so that People who are temperate and laborious have every Chance of bettering their Circumstances. Adds that the price of Bread in the Country he hath left is greatly Enhanced by distilling, that being for so long a time so scarce and dear, and the price of Cattle at the same time reduced full one half while the Rents of lands have been raised nearly in the same proportion, all the smaller Farms must inevitably be ruined.

ELIZ. McDONALD, Aged 29 years, Unmarried, Servant to James
Duncan in (?) Mointle in the Parish of Farr in the
County of Sutherland, Intends to go to Wilmington in
North Carolina; left her own Country because several
of her Friends having gone to Carolina before her, had
assured her that she would get much better Service
and greater Encouragement in Carolina than in her own
Country.

DONALD McDONALD, Aged 29 years, by Trade a Farmer and Taylor,
married, hath one Child Six years Old.   Resided last at
Chapter in the Parish of Rae (sic) in the County of
Caithness upon the Estate of Mr. Alex.r Nicolson Minister
at Thurso, intends to go to Carolina; left his own
Country for the reasons assigned by John Catanock, as he
resided in the same Town and was subjected to the same
Hardships with the other.   Complains as he doth of the
advanced price of Corn, owing in a great measure to
the Consumption of it in Distilling.

JOHN McBEATH, Aged 37, by Trade a Farmer and Shoe maker,
Married, hath 5 Childre from 13 years to 9 months Old.
Resided last in Mault in the Parish of Kildonnan in the
County of Sutherland, upon the Estate of Sutherland,
Intends to go to Wilmington in North Carolina; left his
own Country because Crops failed, he lost his Cattle,

the Rent of his possession was raised, and bread had been
long dear; he could get no employment at home, whereby
he could support himself and Family, being unable to buy
Bread at the prices the Factors on the Estate of Sutherland
& Neighbouring Estates exacted from him. That he was
Encouraged to emigrate by the accounts received from his
own and his Wife's Friends already in America, assuring
him that he would procure comfortable Subsistence in that
Country for his Wife and Children, and that the price of
labour was very high. He also assigns for the Cause of
Bread being dear in his Country that it is owing to the
great quantities of Corn consumed in brewing Risquebah.

JAMES DUNCAN, Aged twenty seven years, by Trade a Farmer,
Married hath two Children, one five years the other 9
months old. Resided last at Moudlein the Parish of Farr
in the Shire of Sutherland, upon the Estate of Sutherland,
Intends to go to Wilmington in North Carolina; Left his
own Country because Crops failed him for several years,
and among the last years of this labouring he scarce reaped
any Crop; Bread became dear and the price of Cattle so
much reduced that one Cows price could only buy a Boll of
Meal. That the People on the Estate of Sutherland were
often supplied with Meal from Caithness, but the Farmers
there, had of late stopt the Sale of their Meal, because

it rendered them a much greater Profit by Distilling.
That he could find no Employment at home whereby he could
support his Family.   That he has very promising Prospects
by the Advices from his Friends in Carolina, as they have
bettered their Circumstances greatly since they went there
by their labour, Lands being cheap and good Provisions
plenty, and the price of Labour very encouraging.

HECTOR McDONALD, Aged 75, Married, a Farmer, hath three Sons
   who emigrate with him, John, Alexander & George, from 27
   to 22 years old.   Also two Grand Children Hector Campbell
   Aged 16, and Alex^r. Campbell Aged 12, who go to their Mother
   already in Carolina.   Resided last at Langwall in the
   Parish of Rogart in the County of Sutherland, upon the
   Estate of Sutherland.   Intends to go to North Carolina,
   Left his own Country because the Rents of his possession
   had been raised from one pound seven shillings to Four
   pounds, while the price of the Cattle raised upon it fell
   more than One half and not being in a Corn Country the
   price of Bread was so far advanced, that a Cow formerly
   worth from 50 sh. to £3 Could only purchase a Boll of Meal.
   He suffered much by the death of Cattle, and still more
   by oppressive Services exacted by the factor, being obliged
   to work with his People & Cattle for 40 days and more
   Each year, without a bit of Bread.   That falling into
   reduced Circumstances he was assured by some of his Children

already in America that his Family might subsist more
comfortably there, and in all events they can scarce be
worse.   Ascribes the excessive price of Corn to the
Consumption of it in Distilling.

WILLIAM McDONALD, Aged 71, by Trade a Farmer, married, hath
3 Children from 7 to 3 Years Old, who emigrate with him.
Resided last at little Savall in the Parish of Lairg in
the County of Sutherland, upon the Estate of Hugh Monro
of Achanny.   Intends to go to Wilmington in North Carolina;
left his own Country because Crops failed, Bread became
dear, the Rents of his possession were raised, but not so
high as the Lands belonging to the Neighbouring Hintors,
by which and the excessive price of Meal, the lowness
of the price of Cattle, and still further by a Cautionary
by which he lost 30£ Sterling, his Circumstances were
much straitened, so that he could no longer support his
Family at Home, tho' Mr. Monro used him with great humanity.
That his Friends already in Carolina, have given him assurances of bettering his Condition, as the price of labour
is very high and Provisions very cheap.   Ascribes the high
price of Corn to the Consumption of it in Distilling.

HUGH MATHESON, Aged 32, Married, hath 3 Children from 8 to 2
Years Old, also a Sister Kathrine Matheson aged 16 who
emigrate with him, was a farmer last at Rumsdale in the

Parish of Kildonan, in the County of Sutherland, Leaves his
Country and goes to Carolina because upon the rise of the
price of Cattle since years ago the Rent of his Possession
was raised from 2.16.0 to 5.10.0 But the price of Cattle
has been of late so low, and that of Bread so high, that
the Factor who was also a Drover would give no more than
a Boll of Meal for a Cow, which was formerly worth from
50sh. to £3 and obliged the Tenants to give him their
Cattle at his own price.   That in these grassing Counties
little Corn can be raised, and for some years past the
little they had was in a great measure blighted and rendered
useless by the frost which is common in the beginning of
Autumn in the Inland parts of the Country.   That in such
Circumstances it seems impossible for Farmers to avoid
Ruin, And their distresses heightened by the Consumption
of Corn in distilling in a grassing Country where little
can be raised.   That encouraged by his Friends already
in America, he hath good hopes of bettering his Condition
in that Country.

Wm. McKAY, Aged 26, Married, a Farmer last at Craigie in the
    Parish of Rae and County of Caithness, upon the Estate
    of George McKay Island hand is;   Goes to Carolina because
    the Rent of his Possession was raised to double at the same
    time that the price of Cattle was reduced one half, and
    even lower as he was obliged to sell them to the Factor at

what price he pleased; At the same time his Crop was
destroyed by bad Harvests, and Bread became excessive
dear, owing in a great measure to the Consumption by
distilling. That the Services were oppressive, being
unlimited and arbitrary, at the pleasure of the Factor;
and when by reason of Sickness the Declarant could not
perform them he was charged at the rate of One Shilling
pday. He had Assurances from his Friends in America that
the high price of Labour and cheapness of Provisions would
enable him to support himself in that Country.

ALEX^r. SINCLAIR, Aged 36, Married, hath 3 Children from 18 to
2 Years Old, a Farmer last at Dollochlagy in the Parish
of Rae and County of Caithness, upon the Estate of Sir
John Sinclair of Murkle. Left his own Country and goes
to Carolina, because the Tacksman of Sir John Sinclairs
Estate, demanded an advanced Rent and arbitrary Services,
which in the present Distresses of the Country could not
be complied with without ruin. That he is encouraged
by his Friends in America to hope to better his Circumstances there.

GEORGE GRANT, Aged twenty, Married, a Farmer last at Aschog
in the Parish of Kildonan in the County of Sutherland on
the Estate of ----- Intends to go to North Carolina,
because Crops failed, so that he was obliged to buy four

Months Provisions in a year, and at the same time the
price of Cattle was reduced more than One half. That
his Brothers in Law already in America have assured him
that from the Cheapness of Provisions, and the high price
of labour, he may better his Circumstances in that Country.

WILLIAM BAIN, Aged 37, a Widower, by Trade a Shopkeeper, resided
last in Wick in the County of Caithness.   Intends to go
to Carolina.   Left his own Country because he could not
get bread in his Employment, the Poverty of the Common
People with whom he dealt disabling them to pay their
debts.   Hopes to better his Condition in America, but
in what business he cannot determine till he comes there.

GEORGE MORGAN,   Aged 37, Married, hath two Children, One 7
the other One year Old, a Farmer last at Chabster in the
Parish of Rae, and County of Caithness, upon lands
belonging to Mr. Alex^r. Nicolson Minister at Thurso.
Goes to Carolina leaving his Country for the same reasons
and upon the same Motives assigned by John Catanock, who
was his Neighbour.

WILL^m. MONRO, Aged thirty four, Married, Emigrates with his
Wife, a Servant Maid, and a Servant Boy, by Trade a Shoemaker,
resided last at Borgymore in the Parish of Tongue, and
County of Sutherland.   Left his own Country as his

Employment was little and he had no hopes of bettering his
Circumstances in it, which he expects to do in America.

PATRICK ROSS, Aged thirty five, Unmarried, lately Schoolmaster
in the Parish of Farr, in the County of Sutherland.
Goes to America on the assurance of some of his Friends
already in that Country of procuring a more profitable
School for him.

ALEX^r. MORISON, Aged Sixty, Married, hath One Son and a
Servant Maid, who emigrate with him, resided last at
Kinside in the Parish of Tongue and County of Sutherland,
on the Estate of Sutherland, by Occupation a Farmer.
Left his Country as the Rents of his Possession were
near doubled, the price of Cattle low, and little being
raised in that Country, what they bought was excessive
dear; beside the Tenans (sic) were in various ways
opprest by Lord Raes Factors; And by the Reports from
America he is in hopes of bettering his Circumstances
in that Country.

GEORGE McKAY, Aged 40, Married, hath one Child, a year old,
by Trade a Taylor and Farmer, last at Strathoolie in the
Parish of Kildonan and County of Sutherland, upon that
part of the Estate of Sutherland set in Tack to George
Gordon by whom his rent was augmented, And great Services

demanded, vizt. 12 days work yearly over and above what he
paid to the Family of Sutherland. That the price of
Cattle on which he chiefly depended was greatly reduced,
and the little Corn raised in the Country almost totally
blighted by Frost for two years past, by which the Farmers
in general were brought into great distress. In these
Circumstances he had no resource but to follow his
Countrymen to America as his Condition can scarce be worse.

DONALD GUN, Aged thirty three, Married, hath three Children
from 8 years to 5 weeks old, by Trade a Taylor, resided
last at Achinnaris in the Parish of Halerick in the
County of Caithness. Finding he cannot make bread in his
own Country, intends to go to America in hopes of doing
it better there.

JOHN ROSS, Aged 47, a Widower hath six Children, from 20 to
5 Years Old, who emigrate with him, by Trade a Farmer, last
at Kabel in the Parish of Farr and County of Sutherland,
upon the Estate of Sutherland. Goes to Carolina, because
the rent of his Possession was greatly Advanced, the price
of Cattle which must pay that Rent reduced more than one
half, and bread which they must always buy excessively dear.
The evil is the greater that the Estate being parcelled
out to different Factors and Tacksmen, these must oppress
the Subtenants, in order to raise a profit to themselves,

particularly on the Article of Cattle, which they never
fail to take at their own prices, lately at 20/- or 20
Merks, and seldom or never higher than 30/- tho' the same
Cattle have been sold in the Country from 50 to 55 sh.
By these means reduced in his Circumstances, and encouraged
by his Friends already in America, he hopes to live
more comfortably in that Country.

JAMES SINCLAIR, Aged twenty one years, a Farmer, married, hath
no children, resided last at Forsenain in the Parish of
Rea, and County of Caithness, upon the Estate of Bighouse
now possest by George McKay of Island handa, upon a Farm,
paying 8ᴸ Sterling Rent, that he left his own Country because
Crops of Corn had failed, and Bread was very dear; he had
lost great part of his Cattle two years ago, the rearing
Cattle being his principal business, the prices of Cattle
were reduced one half while the Rents were nevertheless
kept up and in many places advanced. In such Circumstances
it was not possible for people of small Stocks to evill
ruin. His Father, Brother and Sisters and some other
Friends go along with him to Carolina, where he is informed
land and Provisions are cheap, labour dear, and Crops seldom
fail. What employment he shall follow there he hath
not yet determined, but thinks it will be Husbandry.

AENEAS McLEOD, Aged Sixty, a Farmer, married, hath one Daugher

15 Years Old. Resided last in the Parish of Tongue in
the County of Sutherland upon the Estate of Lord Rae.
Goes to Wilmington in North Carolina where he proposes
to live by day labour, being informed that one days Wages
will support him a week. Left his own Country because
upon the rise of the price of Cattle some years ago, the
Rent of his Possession was raised from 28/- to 38/- a year,
but thereafter when the price of Cattle was reduced one
half, the Rent was nevertheless still kept up. Moreover
being near the house of Tongue, He was harrassed and
oppressed with arbitrary Services daily called for without
Wages or Maintenance.

AENEAS MACKAY, Aged twenty, single, resided last with his Father
in the Parish of Tongue and County of Sutherland; hath
been taught to read, write and cypher, and goes to Carolina
in hopes of being employed either as a Teacher or as a
Clerk; He has several Relations and Acquaintances there
already, who inform him he may get from 60 to 70£ a year
in this way, which is much better than he had any reason to
expect at home.

DONALD CAMPBELL, Aged 50, a Farmer, Married, has One Son 12
years Old; resided last in the Parish of Adrahoolish in
The County of Sutherland on the Estate of Rea. Intends
to go to Carolina because the small Farm he possest (sic)

could not keep a Plough, and he could not raise so much
Corn by delving as maintain his Family and pay his Rent,
which was advanced from 21/- to 30/-. Has hopes of meeting
an Uncle in America who will be able to put him in a way
of gaining his Bread.

Wm. McKAY, Aged 37, a Farmer, Married, has four Children
from 8 years to 18 Months old; and one man Servant, who
emigrate with him, resided last at Strathaledale in the
Parish of Rea, and County of Caithness, upon the Estate
of George McKay of Bighouse. Left his Country because
the Rent of his Possession was raised from 30 to 80L
Scots, while at the same time the price of Cattle upon
which his Subsistence, and the payment of his Rent chiefly
depended had fallen in the last Seven years at least one
half. In the year 1772 he lost of the little Crop his
Farm produced and in Cattle to the value of 40L Sterling.
Under these loses and discouragements, he had assurances
from a Brother and Sister already in Carolina, that a
sober industrious man could not fail of living comfortably,
Lands could be rented cheap, and Ground not cleared
purchased for 6d. an Acre; that the soil was fertile,
and if a man could bring a small Sum of Money with him,
he might make rich very fast. He proposes to follow
Agriculture but has not yet determined, whether he will
purchase or rent a Possession.

WILLIAM McLEOD, Aged twenty six, a Farmer, Married, has one Son
two years old; resided last in the Parish of Adrachoolish,
in the County of Sutherland, upon the Estate of Bighouse;
intends to go to Wilmington in North Carolina, where he has
a Brother settled who wrote him to come out assuring him that
he would find a better Farm for him than he possest at home
(the rent of which was considerably raised upon him) for One
fourth of the Money and that he will live more comfortably
in every respect.

HUGH MONRO, Aged twenty six, a Shoemaker, Married, hath no
Children. Resided last in the Parish of Tongue and
County of Sutherland. Goes to Carolina upon assurance that
Tradesmen of all kinds will find large Encouragement.

WILLᵐ. SUTHERLAND, Aged twenty four, married, left an only Child
at home. Resided last in the Parish of Latheron and County
of Caithness, upon the Estate of John Sutherland of Forse.
Goes to Carolina because he lost his Cattle in 1772, And
for a farm of 40/- Rent, was obliged to perform with his
Family and his Horses so many and so arbitrary Services
to his Landlord at all times of the Year, but especially
in Seed time & Harvest, that he could not in (the) two
years he possest it raise as much Corn as serve his Family
for six Months. That his little Stock daily decreasing,
he was encouraged to go to Carolina, by the assurances of the

fertility of the land, which yields three Crops a year,
by which means Provisions are extremely cheap, Wheat
being sold at 3 Kills. a Boll, Potatoes at 1 sh. So
that one Mans labour will maintain a Family of Twenty
Persons.   He has no Money, therefore proposes to employ
himself as a Day labourer, his Wife can spin & Sew,
and he has heard of many going out in the same way who
are now substantial Farmers.   At any rate he comforts
himself in the hopes that he cannot be worse than he
has been at home.

JAMES McKAY,   Aged 60, a Shoemaker, Married, has one Child,
    Resided last on Lord Raes Estate in Strathnaver.   Left
    his own Country, being exceeding poor, and assured by
    his Friends who contributed among them the Money required
    to pay for his Passage, that he would find better
    Employment in Carolina.

                This and the 20 preceding Pages contain
                the Examination of the Emigrants on board
                the Ships Batchelor of Leith, Alex[r]
                Ramage Master, taken by the officers at
                the Port of Lerwick.

15th April 1774.

(Endorsed)   Report of the Examination of the
Emigrants from the Counties of
Caithness & Sutherland, to North
Carolina.

per Comm^{rs}. L^{t}. 3d, June.   Copy.

(P.R.O.) (T. 47/12)

Port Stornaway:

An Account of the Number of Persons who have
Emigrated to America in the Ship Friendship. Thomas Jann
master for Philadelphia.

Persons Names.	Years.	Quality.	Occupation or Employment.	Former Residence.	*Ports or Places to which they have gone.	On what Account and for what purpose they have left the Country.
John McLeod	15	Tents. Son	Servant to	Galsin		
Angus McLeod	15	do.	do.	Brenish		
John McFarlan	16	do.	do.	Lochs		
Angus McIver	13	do.	do.	Uig		
Kenneth Babie	13	do.	do.	Stornaway		
William Glass	16	do.	do.	do.		
Alexander Cameron	13	do.	do.	Garbost		
Donald Christe	12	do.	do.	Shather		
Rory McKenzie	14	Cooprs. Son	do.	Stornaway		
John Campbel	12	Tents. Son	do.	do.		
Peter McIver	15	do.	do.	Bragir		
Kenneth McAulay	17	do.	do.	Bible		
Duncan McKenzie	16	do.	do.	Coll		
Peter McFarlan	19	do.	do.	Galsin		All Emigrated
Duncan McIver	28	Tennant	do.	Coll		in order to
Margaret McIver	20	dos. Wife	Tents.Wife	do.		procure a
Murdo Morison	17	dos.Son	Servant	Uig		Living
John Watson	18	do.	do.	Bible		abroad, as
Mary McLeod	20	dos.Daughter	do.	Stornway		they were
Annable McIver	28	dos. Wife	Tents.Wife	do.		quite desti-
Mary McKenzie	11	dos.Daughter	Servant	do.		tute of
Kathrin McKenzie	9	do.	do.	do.		Bread at
Christn. McKenzie	3	do.	Child	do.		home.
John McKenzie	18	dos. Son	Servant	Ness		
Neil McLeod	30	Tennant	do.	Melbost		
Margart. Murray	27	dos. Wife	do.	do.		
Christian McLeod	12	dos.Daughter	do.	do.		
Normand McLeod	9	dos.Son	do.	do.		
Margt. McLeod	2	dos.Daughter	do.	do.		
Murdo Christe	9	Tents. Son	do.	Bregair		
Angus McGumri	19	do.	do.	Braynohiy		
Margaret Murray	25	Sailrs.Wife	Sailrs.Wife	Stornaway		

* Philadelphia.

George McLeod	11	dos. Son	Servant	do.	
Malcom McLeod	5	do.	do.	do.	
Jannet McLeod	1	dos. daughter	do.	do.	
John McLeod	33	Tennant	Tennant	Caslova	
Kathrin McIver	30	dos. Wife	dos. Wife	do.	
Margaret McLeod	13	dos. daughter	Servant	do.	
Ann McLeod	10	do. do.	do.	do.	
John McLeod	4	dos.Son	do.	do.	
Malcom McLeod	1	do.	do.	do.	
Finlay McKenzie	45	Cooper	Cooper	Stornaway	
Malcom McLean	24	Tennant	Tennant	Barvis	
Mary McKenzie	45	Cooprs.Wife	Cooprs.Wife	Stornaway	
John McKenzie	10	dos. Son	Servant	do.	
Kathrin McDonald	30	Tents.Daughter	Servant	Coriby	
Ann McLeod	22	do.	do.	Barvis	
Margt. McIver	30	Widow	do.	Shathir	
Margaret Smith	36	do.	do.	Galsin	
Angus McIver	17	Tents. Son	do.	Back	
Finlow Nicolson	16	dos. Son	do.	Bible	
Murdoch Martin	15	do.	do.	Barvis	
Alexander Reid	45	Farmer	Farmer	Broadie	
Kathrine Hutchison	43	dos. Wife	dos. Wife	do.	
Alexander Reid	19	dos. Son	dos. Son	do.	
Mary Reid	17	dos. Daughter	dos.Daughter	do.	
Isobell Reid	15	do. do.	do. do.	do.	
James Reid	13	dos. Son	dos. Son.	do.	All Emigrated
George Reid	10	do. do.	do. do.	do.	for the pre-
David Reid	8	do. do.	do. do.	do.	ceding
Kathrine Reid	6	dos. daughter	dos.Daughter	do.	Reason.
Hindred Reid	2	do. do.	do. do.	do.	
John Reid	½	dos. Son	dos. Son	do.	
Kathrin McIver	13	Tents. Daughr.	Servant	Shathir	
John McIver	9	dos. Son	do.	do.	
Mary McIver	6	dos. Daughr.	do.	do.	
Ann Guin	15	do.	do.	do.	
Christian Guin	13	do.	do.	Galsin	
John Guin	4	dos. Son	do.	do.	
Christian Fraser	25	dos. Daughr.	do.	Stornaway	
Angus McLeod	30	Weaver	Weaver	do.	
Ann McDonald	30	dos. Wife	dos. Wife	do.	
Ann McLeod	2	dos. Daughtr.	dos. Daughr.	do.	
Ann McFarlan	17	Tents.Daughr.	Servant	do.	
Peggie McLeod	20	do.	do.	do.	
Kathrin Murray	21	do.	do.	do.	
Jean McKenzie	20	do.	do.	do.	
Katherin Paterson	16	do.	do.	do.	
Kathrin Nicolson	18	do.	do.	do.	
Ann Crighton	28	do.	do.	do.	
John McMillan	19	Tents. Son	do.	Polue	
Normand Morison	50	Tennant	Tennant	Bragir	
Katherin McKenzie	40	dos. Wife	dos. Wife	do.	

Philadelphia. Port to which they have gone.

Margaret Grant	14	dos. Daugh^r.	Servant	Holm
Katherin Sutherland	27	do.	do.	Stornaway
Alexander Campbell	36	Tennant	do.	Natiskir
Magaret Morison	40	dos. Wife	Tents. Wife	do.
Neil Campbell	17	dos. Son	Servant	do.
Isobel Campbel	6	Tents. Daughter	do.	do.
Willm. McLean	30	Tennant	do.	Bible
Hendred Murray	29	dos. Wife	Tents. Wife	do.
Donald McLean	11	dos. Son	Servant	do.
John McLean	2	do. do.	do.	do.
Normand McAulay	28	Tennant	do.	do.
Isobell McLeod	21	dos. Wife	Tents. Wife	do.
Ann McAulay	2	dos. Daughter	dos. Daughter	do.
Morda McKenzie	30	Tennant	Servant	do.
Donald McKenzie	7	do.	do.	do.
Ann Morison	12	Tents. Daughr.	do.	Ness
Malcom McLeod	18	Tents. Son	do.	Stornaway
Willm. Hutchison	30	Baker	Baker	Nairn
Jannet Mathison	11	Tents. Daugh^r.	Servant	Ness
Normand McLeod	14	Farm^{rs}. Son	do.	Bible
Donald McDonald	11	Tents. Son	Servant	Stornaway
John McDonald	12	do.	do.	do.
Jean McLeod	16	Farmrs. Daughr	Farmrs. Daughr.	Bible

Emigrated for the Preceding Reasons.

Philadelphia. Port to which they have gone.

Men	45
Women	37
Children	24
Total	106

Custom h^o. Stornaway

2nd May 1774.

(Signed) (ARCH. SMITH Coll^r.
(JOHN REID Comp^r.

(Endorsed)

Port Stornway.
An Account of the Number of Persons
who have Emigrated to America
in the Friendship of & for
Philadelphia Thomas Jann
Master - 1774.

(P.R.O.) (T. 47/12)   List of Passengers in the Gale of Whitehaven for New York.

Time of Entry.	Ship's name.	Master's Name.	Where Bound.	Passengers Names.	From what place.	Age	Occupation.	Reasons for going.
1774 May 7th.	Gale	Heny. Jiferson	New York.	Wm. McCartney	Queenshill	20 years	husband-)man)	Want of Employment.
				Alexr. McMurray	do.	26 do.	ditto	ditto
				James Carson	do.	19 do.	ditto	ditto.
				Alexr. McNaught	Largs of) Twineholm)	23 do.	do.	do.
				5 John McNaught	ditto	20 ditto	ditto	ditto
				Alexr. Bryce	Kirkbride) Anwoth)	46 ditto	ditto	ditto
				Mary Bryce	ditto	36 ditto		ditto
				Jane Bryce	ditto	9 months		
				Thos. Carson	Gatehouse	36 years	Brewer	ditto
				10 John Herron	ditto	16 ditto	Joiner	ditto
				James Herron	ditto	12 ditto		ditto
				John Ramsay	ditto	12 ditto		ditto
				Wm. Manson	Ferrytown	30 ditto	Labourer	do.
				James Hannah	Gatehouse	17 do.	Taylor	do.
				15 James Murray	do.	20 do.	Labourer	do.
				John Carson	do.	18 do.	do.	do.
				Andr. Hannah	do.	40 do.	do.	do.
				John McGoughtrey	do.	40 do.	Farmer	do.
				Richd.McGoughtry	do.	68 do.	do.	do.
				20 Jas. McGoughtry	do.	17 do.	Mason	do.
				Geo. Liviston	do.	22 do.	do.	do.
				James Selkirk	do.	22 do.	Taylor	do.
				John McGoughtry	do.	16 do.	Labourer	do.
				Alexr.McGoughtry	do.	7 do.		do.
				22 John Rudderford	Tungland	8 do.		
				Mary Couchtry	Gatehouse	15 do.		do.
				Margt.McGoughtry	Girthon	21 do.		do.
				Jane McGoughtry	do.	2 do.		

No.	Name	Place	Age		Occupation	
30	James Herron	Gatehouse	40	do.	Mason	do.
	Robt. Herron	do.	14	do.	Mason	do.
	Saml. Herron	do.	22	do.		do.
	Mary Milligan	do.	34	do.		do.
	Agnes Milligan	do.	31	do.		do.
	James Manson	do.	36	do.		do.
35	Saml. Ramsay	do.	46	do.	Joiner	do.
	Wm. Ramsay	do.	8	do.		do.
	Dorothy Ramsay	do.	18	do.		
	Cathrine Hannah	do.	26	do.		
	Andw. Hannah	do.	2	do.		
40	Elizt. Ramsay	do.	3	do.		
	Wm. McGoughtry	do.	6	do.		
	Eliz. Hannay	do.	7	do.		
	Agnes McGoughtry	do.	8	do.		
	Jane Ramsay	do.	3	do.		
45	Margt. Ramsay	do.	2	do.		
	James Hannah	do.	6	do.		
	Jane Ramsay	do.	20	do.		do.
	Geo. Ramsay	do.	7	do.		do.
	John McMillan	Balmaghie	36	do.		do.
50	John Hannay	Gatehouse	7	do.		do.
	Eliz. Carson	Balmaghie	26	do.		do.
	Agnes Gordon	Queenshill	26	do.		do.
	James McMillan	Balmaghie	12	do.		do.
	Eliz. Gordon	do.	20	do.		
55	James McMillan	do.	10	do.		
	Janet McMillan	do.	8	do.		
	Agnes McMillan	do.	6	do.		
	Eliz. McMillan	do.	4	do.		
	Elis. Ganworth	Aimworth	25	do.		
60	Wm. Bryce	do.	3 months			do.
61	Margt. Deniston	Kirkcudbright	36 years			
	John Rutherford	do.	8	do.		

(P.R.O.)   (R. 47/12)

Port Greenock. (List of Passengers from the 13th May 1774
(Inclusive to the 20th May 1774 Exclusive.

	Names.	Age.	Former Residence.	Employment.	Whither Bound	*Oh what account and for what purpose they go.	**In what Ship.
1	Robert Grant	47	Strathspey	Farmer	New York		
2	Mary Grant	43	"		"		
3	Alex^r. Grant	24	"	Do.	"		
4	Eliza Grant	20	"		"		
5	Peter Grant	17	"	Do.	"		
6	Katherine Grant	10	"		"		
7	Donald Grant	8	"		"		
8	George Grant	6	"		"		
9	Fanny Frant	4	"		"		
10	Margaret Grant	3	"		"		
11	Elen Grant	2	"		"		
12	James Stewart	22	"	Do.	"		
13	Jean Grant	17	"		"		
14	John Stewart	35	"	Do.	"		
15	James Stewart	31	"	Do.	"		
16	Mary Stewart	14	"		"		
17	George Stewart	10	"		"		
18	Henry Stewart	7	"		"		
19	Gilbert Stewart	4	"		"		
20	John Grant	42	"	Do.	"		
21	Margery Grant	39	"	Do.	"		
22	Peter Grant	19	"	Do.	"		
23	Donald Grant	17	"	Do.	"		
24	Eliza Grant	15	"		"		
25	Elspa Grant	14	"		"		
26	Nelly Grant	11	"		"		
27	Alex^r. Grant	10	"		"		
28	Jannet Grant	8	"		"		
29	James Grant	47	"	Do.	"		
30	Ann Grant	44	"		"		
31	Jannet Grant	23	"		"		
32	Ann Grant	21	"		"		
33	James Grant	20	"	Do.	"		
34	Sally Grant	17	"		"		
35	Margery Grant	14	"		"		
36	Peter Grant	10	"		"		
37	William Grant	52	"		"		
38	Ann Grant	49	"		"		

* High Rents & Deerness of Provisions.

** In the "George" of Greenock. Arch^d. Bog Master for New York.

39 Barbara Grant	27	Strathspey		New York
40 William Grant	22	"		"
41 Peter Grant	20	"	Do.	"
42 Peter Grant	18	"	Do.	"
43 Ann Grant	15	"		"
44 Margery Grant	9	"		"
45 Jannet Grant	6	"		"
46 John Grant	2	"		"
47 Robert Grant	1½	"		"
48 Alexr. Cameron	32	"	Do.	"
49 Jean Cameron	29	"		"
50 Jannet Cameron	5	"		"
51 Elspa Cameron	2	"		"
52 Jean Cameron	2	"		"
53 John Stewart	23	"	Do.	"
54 James Cumming	19	"	Do.	"
55 James Houston	27	"	Do.	"
56 Robert Grant	29	"	Do.	"
57 Alexr. Grant	25	"	Do.	"
58 Ann Grant	18	"		"
59 Duncan Mackenzie	22	"	Do.	"
60 Alexr. Cumming	29	"	Do.	"
61 David Grant	46	"	Do.	"
62 George Grant	24	"	Do.	"
63 John Grant	19	"	Do.	"
64 John Mackenzie	25	"	Do.	"
65 James Grant	23	"	Do.	"
66 James Warrand	24	"	Do.	"
67 Patrick Grant	29	"	Do.	"
68 James Grant	27	"	Do.	"
69 James Cameron	32	"	Do.	"
70 John Cameron	21	"	Do.	"
71 Jean Cameron	19	"		"
72 Wm. Cumming	52	"	Do.	"
73 Isobell Cumming	48	"		"
74 Margaret Cumming	28	"		"
75 Barbra Cumming	26	"		"
76 Margery Cumming	23	"		"
77 Isobell Cumming	19	"		"
78 Alexr. Cumming	14	"		"
79 Katherine Cumming	12	"		"
80 John Cumming	10	"		"
81 John MacDonald	48	"		"
82 Jean McDonald	44	"		"
83 Henereta McDonald	21	"		"
84 Jannet MacDonald	19	"		"
85 Alexr. MacDonald	14	"		"
86 Elspa MacDonald	10	"		"
87 William MacKenzie	17	"	Do.	"
88 Allan Grant	22	"	Do.	"

(High Rents & Deerness of Provisions)

(In the "George" of Greenock. Archd. Bog Master for New York.)

89	John Cumming	16	Strathspey	Do.	New York
90	Katherine Cumming	10	"		"
91	And^w. Bain	23	"	Farmer	"
92	Isobell Bain	17	"		"
93	John Duncan	44	"	Do.	"
94	Ann Duncan	31	"		"
95	Isobell Duncan	29	"		"
96	Jean Duncan	17	"		"
97	Katherine Duncan	5	"		"
98	James Duncan	2½	"		"
99	William Duncan	1	"		"
100	Donald Cumming	45	"	Do.	"
101	Elspa Cumming	41	"		"
102	Mary Cumming	10	"		"
103	Alex^r. Cumming	9	"		"
104	Peter Cumming	7	"		"
105	John Cumming	2½	"		"
106	Margery Cumming	1	"		"
107	James Bain	32	"	Do.	"
108	Christian Bain	27	"		"
109	Ann Bain	10	"		"
110	William Bain	8	"		"
111	Alex^r. Bain	4	"		"
112	Isobell Bain	3	"		"
113	James Calder	18	"	Do.	"
114	Marg^t. Calder	24	"	Do.	"
115	John McKay	18	"	Do.	"
116	James Mitchell	22	"	Do.	"
117	Mary Mitchell	25	"		"
118	John Mitchell	4	"		"
119	Mary Grant	12	"		"
120	John McDonald	22	"	Do.	"
121	Margery McDonald	20	"		"
122	Mary Cumming	6	"		"
123	Alex^r. Watson	35	"	Do.	"
124	Lewis Grant	32	"	Do.	"
125	James Grant	47	"	Do.	"
126	Mrs. Grant	39	"		"
127	Alex^r. Grant	29	"	Do.	"
128	Swithen Grant	8	"		"
129	Betty Grant	6	"		"
130	Marry Grant	3	"		"
131	Francis Grant	2	"		"
132	Peter McAlpin	48	Inverness	Do.	"
133	Eliza McAlpin	42	Do.		"
134	John Cumming	34	Strathspey	Do.	"
135	Mrs. Cumming	24	Do.		"
136	John McPherson	42	Greenock	Shipmaster	" (To push his fortune.

(High Rents & Deerness of Provisions.)

(In the "George" of Greenock. Arch^d. Bog Master for New York.)

No.	Name	Age	Origin	Occupation	Destination	Reason	Notes
137	Mrs. McPherson	28	Greenock		New York	High Rents and Want of Employ	In the "George" of Greenock. Archd, Bog Master for New York
138	Robt. Summers	27	Elgin	Joiner			
139	Barthw. Summers	25	Do.	Butcher			
140	George Square	29	Aberdeen	Mason			
141	Gilbert McNeil	21	Kilmar-) nock)	Merchant			
142	Ann Ross	20	Kilsyth				
143	James Hamilton	41	Paisley	Farmer			
144	Rachell Ross	29	Do.				
145	Saml. Aitken	24	Inverness	Farmer			
146	James McCaul	20	Do.	Do.			
147	James Fulton	21	Do.	Do.			
148	Agnes Cunningham	24	Do.	Do.			
149	Wm. McKay	23	Do.	Taylor			
150	James Scrimiger	29	Greenock	Mariner			
151	Alexr. Wilson	24	Do.	Do.			
152	John Ferguson	27	Paisley	Weaver			
153	Jannet Burnet	21	Do.				
154	Robt. Hendry	22	Dundee	Taylor			
155	John Addison	26	Glasgow	Preacher			
156	Donald Morrison	25	Stornway	Cooper			
157	Allan Beatton	18	Dundee	Butcher			
158	Andw. Wilson	24	Aberdeen	Taylor			
159	Isobell Smith	25	Crawfords-) dyke)				
160	Isobell McArthur	27	Do.				
161	Alexr. Morison	32	Aberdeen	Mason			
162	Mary Morison	34	Do.				
163	Hugh Ross	17	Strathspey	Farmer			
164	William Ross	14	Do.	Do.			
165	Margt. Allan	29	Do.				
166	James Ross	30	Do.	Do.			
167	John Ross	24	Do.	Do.			
168	Agness McGriger	26	Do.				
169	John Caddell	25	Perth	Mason			
170	Joseph Baillie	20	York	Cutler			
171	George Paterson	21	Kilsyth	Farmer			
172	David Muir	19	Do.	Do.			
173	John Murdock	25	Stirling	Farmer		High Rents	
174	Donald Ferguson	20	Do.	Do.		Do.	
175	William Aitken	30	Perth	Do.		Do.	
176	William Mathew	25	Air	Shoe-)maker)	New York	To follow his business	In the "Matty" of Greenock Thomas Cochrane Ma. for New York
177	John Mathew	24	Do.	Do.			
178	Robert Robertson	30	Glasgow	Weaver		Do.	
179	Mrs. Robertson.	25	Do.				
180	Alexr. Cowan	20	Do.	Do.		Do.	
181	James Fergus	24	Do.	Do.		Do.	
182	Wm. Stirling	28	Do.	Do.			
183	Mrs. Stirling	24	Do.				

184 John Stirling	6	Do.		New York	In the "Matty"
185 May Stirling	2	Do.			of Greenock.
166 Henry Crawford	25	Paisley	Do.		Do. Thomas
187 Arch^d. Nisbert	27	Stirling	Farmer		Do. Cochrane Ma.
188 Alex^r. Comney	24	Do.	Do.		Do. for New York.
189 Robert Anderson	25	Do.	Do.		Do.
190 Thomas Clerk	28	Do.	Do.		Do.
191 Robt. Barkley	23	Do.	Do.		Do.
192 Wm. Gillispie	20	Do.	Do.		Do.
193 Jas. McGown	25	Do.	Do.		Do.
194 Mrs. McGown	29	Do.			Do.
195 Marg^t. McGown	20	Do.			Do.
196 John Reid	25	Do.	Do.		Do.
197 John Graham	25	Do.	Do.		Do.
198 Alex^r. Harvie	28	Do.	Do.		Do.
199 John Clerk	25	Do.	Do.		Do.
200 Jas. Ferguson	20	Do.	Do.		Do.
201 John Galbreath	20	Do.	Do.		Do.
202 John Mitchell	25	Glasgow	Do.		Do.
203 Wm. Bell	29	Do.	Do.		Do.
204 Mrs. Paul	25	Do.			Do.
205 Jas. Whitelaw	25	Do.	Do.		Do.
206 John Paul	29	Do.	Do.		Do.
207 Marg^t. Paul	2	Do.			Do.
208 James Watson	30	Stirling	Do.		Do.
209 Mrs. Watson	25	Do.	Do.		Do.
210 Wm. Bell	25	Paisley	Do.		Do.
211 Mrs. Bell	30	Do.			Do.
212 John Bell	25	Do.	Do.		Do.
213 Alex^r. McIver	21	Glasgow	Merchant		Do.
214 John Walker	21	Do.	Weaver		Do.
215 Mathew Bain	25	Do.	Wright		Do.
216 David Morison	25	Do.	Do.		Do.
217 Alex^r. Young	25	Do.	Do.		Do.
218 Chas. Burt	26	Do.	Do.		Do.
219 Wm. Steel	30	Do.	Labourer		Do.
220 David Dickson	20	Do.	Do.		Do.
221 John Reid	20	Do.	Cooper		Do.
222 Gilbert Mitchell	21	Do.	Rope Maker		Do.
223 Marg^t. Roberts	25	Do.			Do.
224 James Bryson	28	Do.	Farmer		Do.

JOHN DUNLOP.

ALEX CAMPBELL D. Comr.
JO CLERK D. Comr.

(Endorsed)

Port Greenock list of Passengers from the
13th May 1774 inclusive to the 20th May 1774
exclusive.

(P.R.O.) (T. 47/12)

Port Kirkcudbright.   List of Emigrants shiped on board the
Adventure of Liverpool William Landon
Master for New York in America.

Names.	Trade.	Age.	Residence.	Parish.	Reasons for Emigration.
Thomas Sproat	Joiner	36 Years	Kirkcudbright	Kirkcudbright	Want of) Employment.)
Janet Smith		32	do.	do.	
Hugh Sproat	Farmer	27	do.	do.	Do.
Robert Heckle	Mason	34	do.	do.	Do.
Margt. McKittrick		32	do.	do.	
David Heckle		10	do.	do.	
William Heckle		7	do.	do.	
Thos. Heckle		3	do.	do.	
Robt. Heckle		1	do.	do.	
John Kinner	Porter	30	do.	do.	Do.
Nicholas Murray		32	do.	do.	
Anthony Kinner		10	do.	do.	
Eliz. Kinner		7	do.	do.	
Nicholas Kinner		4	do.	do.	
John Rain	Labourer	35	do.	do.	Do.
Eliz. McWhinnie		28	do.	do.	
Thos. Rain		2	do.	do.	
Adam Gordon	Labourer	36	Barwhinoch	Twynholm	Do.
Ann Bryce		31	do.	do.	
Hugh Gordon		10	do.	do.	
Agnes Gordon		7	do.	do.	
Mary Gordon		3	do.	do.	
Edward McMorran	Merchant	25	Dumfries	Dumfires	out of) business.)
Will. McAdam	Taylor	28	Boreland	Balmaghie	want of Employ.
Robert McWhae	Milwright	29	Genoch	do.	Do.
Sam. Denniston	Taylor	25	Auchemairn	Berrick	Do.
John Sproat	Labourer	23	Miln of) Borgue)	Borgue	Do.
Will. Gordon	Do.	22		Twynholm	Do.
John McKie		17	at Water) of orr)	Colvend	to settle) abroad.)
Will. Lindsay	Cabinet) maker)	26	Boreland	Do.	Do.
Peter McRobert	Farmer	38	Drumlanrick	Durisdeer	to view some) lands.)

```
In all                          31

    Shipped at Dumfries          3

    Shipped at Wigton           27

at Do. Children on the breast    5
                                66 Total
```

N.B. Two men & their wives Shipped at Wigton
Indented for four years - and two men
for three years.

(Letter Endorsed)   16 May 1774.

        Mr. Nelthorpe

            List of Persons lately sailed

            as Emigrants from the Pt.

R. 22 May 1774. J.R.   of Kirkcudbright.

Port Stranraer. An Account of Emigrants shipped at Stranraer the 16th May 1774 on board the "Gale" of Whitehaven Henry Jefferson Master for New York in North America, with a Description of their Age, Quality, Occupation, Employment, former Residence, on what Account and for what Purposes they leave the Country.

No.	Emigrants Names.	Ages Years.	Occupation or Employment.	Former Residence.	To what Port or Place Bound.	On what Account and for what Purposes they leave the Country.
1	Wm. Biggam	40	Farmer	Galloway	New) York.)	Hopes to do better.
2	David Maxwell	34	Taylor	do.	do.	do.
3	Jean McGarvin	34		do.	do.	
4	Marion Maxwell	8		do.	do.	
5	Alexr. McComb	21	Husbandman	Glenluce	do.	Cannot tell.
6	Agnes McAwan	23		do.	do	Because she sees) others leaving it.)
7	Alexr. McMicken	23	Farmer	do.	do.	Hopes for better.
8	James McWilliam	23	do.	Galloway	do.	To bear his) Friends Company.)
9	Margt. McMillan	25		do.	do.	
10	Agnes Adair	25		Glenluce	do.	Cannot get a) Husband.)
11	Patrick Adair	50	Farmer	do.	do.	Goes with his) Children.)
12	Andrew Torburn	7		do.	do.	
13	Jean Adair	25		do.	do.	
14	William McQueen	25	Husbandman	do.	do.	To do better.
15	William Adair	17	Labourer	do.	do.	do.
16	Alexander McDouall	40	do.	Galloway	do.	Refused to give a) Reason.)
17	Eliza. McWilliam	35		do.	do.	
18	Edw. McDowall	9		do.	do.	
19	Robert McDowall	7		do.	do.	
20	Thos. McKissack	26	Farmer	Girvan	do.	Hopes for better.
21	Robt. Alexander	25	House) Carpenter)	Dailly	do.	do.
22	Will. McMicken	25	Labourer	do.	do.	Expects to go to) a better Country.)
23	Jean Gauley	25		do.	do.	
24	John Ell	40	Labourer	Cavin	do.	Want of business.
25	William Ell	15		do.	do.	do.
26	Peter Kelly	40		Glenluce	do.	To do better.

27	Ann Adair	26		do.	do.	
28	Jean Kelly	10		do.	do.	
29	Eliza. Kelly	5		do.	do.	
30	Alexander Kelly	8		do.	do.	
31	Jean Campbell	20		Calloway	do.	
32	Anthony McQueeston	18	Baker	do.	do.	Want of Business.
33	Alexander Kelly	22	Labourer	do.	do.	do.
34	John Cumming	26	Taylor	Air	do.	do.
35	William Mean	21	do.	ditto	do.	Hopes for better.
36	Eliza. Macmaster	21		Galloway	do.	
37	Elianora McMicken	25		do.	do.	
38	Janet McMicken	21		do.	do.	
39	Samuel McKie	26	Weaver	do.	do.	Want of Employment.
40	Margaret McKie	26		do.	do.	
41	George McWilliam	25	Husbandman	do.	do.	Dear Land.
42	Will. McCann	35	Weaver	do.	do.	Reported he would do) better in America.)
43	Jean McCann	27		do.	do.	
44	Sarah McCann	8		do.	do.	
45	John McCann	6		do.	do.	
46	Jannet McCann	4		do.	do.	
47	Robt. Bruce	22	Gardner	Galloway	do.	Cannot make a living.
48	Alexr. McDougall	21	do.	do.	do.	do.
49	Alexr. McComb	21	Husbandman	do.	do.	do.
50	Robt. Kelly	38	do.	do.	do.	do.
51	Margt. Kelly	9		do.	do.	
52	Mary Kelly	38		do.	do.	
53	James Kelly	6		do.	do.	
54	Jean Kelly	3		do.	do.	
55	John McWilliam	25	Farmer	do.	do.	Want of Business.
56	John Shaw	23	Smith	do.	do.	For Company's Sake.
57	Alexander Agnew	40	Husbandman	do.	do.	Has no Reason.
58	Janet Agnew	40		do.	do.	
59	Forbes Agnew	18	Labourer	do.	do.	
60	William Agnew	15	do.	do.	do.	
61	John Millroy	40	Farmer	do.	do.	Want of Employment.
62	Eliza. Millroy	36		do.	do.	
63	Mary Millroy	12		do.	do.	
64	Janet Millroy	10		do.	do.	
65	Eliza. Millroy	8		do.	do.	
66	Anthony Millroy	7		do.	do.	
67	John Millroy	6		do.	do.	
68	Agnes Millroy	2		do.	do.	
69	James McWilliam	24	Mason	do.	do.	Want of Business.
70	John McKackey	25	Smith	do.	do.	Want of Employment.
71	John Campbell	22	Taylor	do.	do.	do.
72	John Gibson	19	Farmer	do.	do.	Has no Reason.
73	Jo. Buchannan	58	do.	do.	do.	Curiosity.
74	Michael McKinly	40	do.	do.	do.	For Bread.
75	Jean McKinly	26		do.	do.	
76	John McMicking	21	Farmer	do.	do.	Want of Employment.
77	Thomas McMicking	24	do.	do.	do.	do.
78	Thos. Millwane	17	do.	do.	do.	do.

79	Mary Millwane	25		do.	do.	
80	James McMiking	18	Farmer	do.	do.	To make a Fortune.
81	Patrick Blane	34	do.	do.	do.	Dear Land.
82	Eliza. Blain	30		do.	do.	
83	Jean Blain	8		do.	do.	
84	Jenny Blain	2		do.	do.	
85	Hugh Alexander	45	Carpenter	do.	do.	Land so high not) able to make a living.)
86	Agnes Alexander	30		do.	do.	
87	John Alexander	10		do.	do.	
88	Ann Alexander	10		do.	do.	
89	Hugh Alexander	7		do.	do.	
90	Alexander Alexander	5		do.	do.	
91	James Alexander	3		do.	do.	
92	Robert Alexander	1		do.	do.	
93	John McHaig	36	Farmer	do.	do.	Want of Employment.
94	Grizzel McHaig	26		do.	do.	
95	Margt. McHaig	2		do.	do.	
96	Ann McHaig	4 m.		do.	do.	
97	John Mikine	40	Joiner	do.	do.	To do better.
98	Rosina McMikine	36		do.	do.	
99	Janet McKissack	56		do.	do.	
100	Rosina McMikine	9		do.	do.	
101	Agnes McMikine	7		do.	do.	
102	May McMikine	6		do.	do.	
103	Jean McMikine	5		do.	do.	
104	Nanny McMikine	1		do.	do.	
105	Margt. Gibson	24		do.	do.	
106	Andw. Campbell	34	Shoemaker	do.	do.	Want of Employment.
107	Agnes Campbell	33		do.	do.	
108	Jean Campbell	4		do.	do.	
109	Mary Ann Campbell	1		do.	do.	
110	John Galloway	22	Joiner	do.	do.	Want of Employment.
111	Sarah Galloway	20		do.	do.	
112	Thos. Biggam	40	Weaver	do.	do.	Want of Employment.
113	Mary Biggam	33		do.	do.	
114	Andrew Biggam	9		do.	do.	
115	Jean Biggam	4		do.	do.	
116	Robert McMaster	24	Merchant	do.	do.	Want of Business.
117	Janus Boyd	32	do.	do.	do.	
118	Jean Boyd	22		do.	do.	
119	Thos. McClumpha	26	Farmer	do.	do.	Want of Employment.
120	John McMaster	20	Housewright	do.	do.	do.
121	John Millroy	30	Shoemaker	do.	do.	Want of Employment.
122	Sarah Millroy	26		do.	do.	
123	Jas. McTaggart	20	Labourer	do.	do.	Want of Employment.
124	Wm. Linn	21	do.	do.	do.	Curiosity.
125	John Kennedy	22	do.	do.	do.	Hopes to be better.
126	Wm. Stewart	22	Housewright	do.	do.	Want of Business.
127	Jean McClumpha	22		do.	do.	
128	John McClumpha	2		do.	do.	

129	Alexr. Ross	32	Carpenter	do.	do.	Want of Employment.
130	Jean Ross	30		do.	do.	
131	Isabell Ross	4		do.	do.	
132	Jean Ross	2		do.	do.	
133	Margaret Ross	8 m.		do.	do.	
134	William Beatty	40	Labourer	do.	do.	Want of Employment.
135	Agnes Beatty	40		do.	do.	
136	Mary Beatty	16		do.	do.	
137	Jean Maxwell	32		do.	do.	
138	John Maxwell	2		do.	do.	
139	James McMicken	4		do.	do.	
140	Will. McMicken	2		do.	do.	
141	Jean McKie	2		do.	do.	
142	Janet McWilliam	27		do.	do.	
143	William Angus	24	Labourer	do.	do.	Want of Business.
144	Anthony Milroy		do.	do.	do.	do.
145	James Clark		Waiter	do.	do.	Having run away) with a young Widow) & left a wicked) Wife thought shame) to appear.)
146	Hugh McCrea		Labourer	do.	do.	To do better.
147	Henry Long		do.	do.	do.	Want of Employment.

Customhouse Stranraer 1st June 1774.

N.B. As all the married Women follow their Husbands,
the Girls and Boys their Parents; we have inserted
no Reason for their leaving the Country after their
Names.

(Signed)   (JOHN CLUGSTON Collr.
            (PATK. McINTIRE Compr.

(P.R.O.) (T. 47/12)

Port Greenock. List of Passengers on board the Ship "Ulysses"
James Chalmers Masr. for Wilmington in North Carolina.

Passengers Names.	Age.	Former Place of Residence.	Business.	Reasons for Emigrating.
Robt. McNicol	30	Glenurcha	A Gentn.	High Rents and Oppression.
Jean Campbell his) Wife)	24	Do.	his Wife	
Annapel McNicol) their Daugr.)		Do.		
Abram Hunter	28	Greenock	Shipmaster	To build.
Thomas Young	21	Glasgow	Surgeon	To follow his Trade.
John McNicol	24	Glenurcha	a Workman	High Rents & Oppression.
Angus Galbreath	30	Do.	Do.	Poverty occasion'd by) want of work.)
Katrine Brown his) Wife)	26			Do.
Angus Fletcher	46	Do.	Farmer	High Rents & Oppression.
Katrine McIntyre) his Wife.)	40	Do.		Do.
Euphame Fletcher)	10	Do.		Do.
Mary Fletcher)	6	Do.	their Children	
Nancy Fletcher) their Children)	3	Do.		Do.
John McIntyre	45	Do.	Farmer	Do.
Mary Downie	35	Do.	his Wife	Do.
Nancy McIntyre)	11	Do.		Do.
Christy McIntyre)	8	Do.	their Children	Do.
John McIntyre)	5	Do.		Do.
Duncan McIntyre	40	Do.	Farmer	Do.
Katrine McIntyre	28	Do.	his wife	Do.
John Sinclair	32	Do.	Farmer	Do.
Mary Sinclair	32	Do.	his wife	Do.
Donald McIntyre	28	Do.	Farmer	Do.
Mary McIntyre	25	Do.	his wife	Do.
Dond. McFarlane	26	Do.	Farmer	Do.
Dond. McFarlane	6	Do.	his Son	Do.
Duncan Sinclair	24	Do.	Farmer	Do.
Isobel McIntyre	24	Do.	his wife	Do.
John McIntyre	35	Do.	Farmer	Do.
Margt. McIntyre	30	Do.	his wife	Do.
Malcom McPherson	40	Do.	Farmer	Do.
Chistn. (sic) Downie	30	Do.	his wife	Do.
Janet McPherson	10)	Do.	their Children	Do.
Wm. McPherson	9)			Do.

Name	Age	Place	Occupation	Cause
Willm. Picken	32	Do.	Farmer	Do.
Martha Huie	26	Do.	his wife	Do.
Robt. Howie	18	Do.	Workman	Poverty Occasion'd by) want of work.
Archd. McMillan	58	Do.	Farmer	High Rents & Oppression.
Mary Taylor	40	Do.	his wife	Do.
Barbra McMillan	20	Do.	their Daugr.	Do.
John Greenlees	25	Kintyre	Farmer	Do.
Mary Howie	25	Do.	his wife	Do.
Peter McArthur	58	Do.	Farmer	Do.
Chrisn. Bride	52	Do.	his wife	Do.
John McArthur	16)	Do.		
Ann McArthur	38)	Do.	their Children	
Joan McArthur	20)	Do.		
John McArthur	18)	Do.		
Dond. Caldwell	18	Do.	Shoemaker	Poverty Occasion'd by) want of work.)
Robt. Mitchell	26	Do.	Taylor	Do.
Ann Campbell	26	Do.	his wife	Do.
Alexr. Callan	22	Do.	Workman	Do.
Juer McMillan	26	Do.	Farmer	High Rents & Oppression.
Jean Huie	23	Do.	his wife	Do.
John Ferguson	19	Do.	Workman	Poverty Occasion'd by) want of work.)
Robt. McKiehan	32	Do.	Farmer	High Rents & Oppression.
Janet McKendrick	24	Do.	his wife	Do.
Neil McKiehan	5	Do.	their Son	Do.
Malm. McMillan	58	Kintyre	Farmer	High Rents and Oppression.
Cathn. McAlester	58		his wife	
Daniel McMillan	24)			Do.
Archd. McMillan	16)		their Children	Do.
Gilbt. McMillan	8)			Do.
Dond. McKay	20)		Taylor	Do.
Danl. Campbell	25		Farmer	Do.
Andw. Hyndman	46		do.	Do.
Cathn. Campbell	46		his wife	Do.
Mary Hyndman	18)			
Margt. Hyndman	14)		their Children	Do.
Angus Gilchrist	25)			
Malm. Smith	64		Farmer	Do.
Mary McAlester	64		his wife	Do.
Peter Smith	23)		their Children	Do.
Mary Smith	19)			Do.
Duncan McAllum	22	Do.	Shoemaker	Do.
Cathn. McAlester	30	Do.	his wife	Do.
Neil Thomson	23	Do.	Farmer	Do.
David Beaton	28	Do.	Do.	Do.
Flora Bride	29	Do.	his wife	Do.
John Gilchrist	25	Do.	Cooper	Do.
Marion Taylor	21	Do.	his wife	Do.
Neil McNeil	64	Do.	Farmer	Do.
Isobel Simpson	64	Do.	his wife	Do.

Danl. McNeil	28)	Do.		Do.-
Hector McNeil	24)	Do.		Do.
Peter McNeil	22)	Do.	Their Children	Do.
Neil McNeil	18)	Do.		Do.
Willm. McNeil	15)	Do.		Do.
Mary McNeil	9)	Do.		Do.
Allan Cameron	28	Do.	Farmer	Do.
Angus Cameron	18	Do.	Do.	Do.
Katrine Cameron	21	Do.	his wife	Do.

ALEXr. CAMPBELL D. Compr.   JO. CLERK D. Collr.

JOHN DUNLOP T.S.

P. Greenock

The above List of Passengers is from the

12th August 1774 Incl. to the 18th Augt. 1774 Excl.

44 .

(P.R.O.) (T. 47/12)

List of Passengers from the 19th August

Port Greenock.   exclusive, till the 25th August inclusive

1774. On board the "Magdelene" James Wallace

Mas^r. for Philadelphia.

Names.	Former Residence.	Occupation & Employment.	Age.	On what Account and for what Business they go.	To what Place bound.
James Christy	Dunbarton	Weaver	59	to follow his Business	Philadelphia
Walter Reid	Dundee	Wright	15	do.	do.
John Stewart	do.	do.	20	do.	do.
John Henderson	Jamaica	Surgeon	23	do.	do.
John Low	Donaghadee	Taylor	19	do.	do.
Andrew Brown	Dumfries	Gentleman	45	for his Health	do.
Walter Murray	Banff	Taylor	22	do.	do.
Archibald McFee	do.	Shoemaker	29	to follow his Business	do.
John Taylor	Argyle) Shire)	Brick-) layer)	25	do.	do.
James Gray	do.	Black-) smith)	21	do.	do.
James Cuthbert	Lanark	do.	19	do.	do.
Margaret Cuthbert	do.	to follow) her Husbd.)	20	to wait her Husband.	do.
Hugh Bollon	Salt) Coats)	Sailor	24	to Study Farming.	do.
Hugh Rankin	do.	Barber	22	to follow his Business	do.
John Johnston	Couper of) Angus)	Cooper	25	do.	do.
James Allan	Greenock	Labourer	27	do.	do.
Lawrence Stoddart	do.	do.	24	do.	do.
Thomas Baird	No.Carolina	Sailor	26	do.	do.
Thomas Etton	Edinburgh	Chapman	26	do.	do.
James Anderson	Glasgow	Wright	21	do.	do.
Alexander Gilmour	do.	Weaver	45	do.	do.
Thomas Wyllie	Dalry	do.	39	do.	do.
George Burns	Alnwick	Gentleman	26	Mercht. Business.	do.
William Chalmers	do.	Butcher	22	to follow his Business.	do.

(Signed)   (JO. CLERK D. Collr.
(A. FV⟨ ⟩ CAMPBELL D. Comptr
(JOHN DUNLOP T.S.

(P.R.O.) (T. 47/12)

Port Greenock. List of Passengers from this Port from the 8th September 1774 inclusive, to the 15th September 1774 exclusive.

Names.	Former Residence.	Occupation or Employment.	Age.	To what Port or Place Bound.	*On what Account and for what Purpose they go.	**In what Ship they take their Passage.
William McDonald	Kintyre	Farmer	40	Wilmington North Carolina	))	
Isobell Wright	do.		36	"		
Mary McDonald	do.		4	"		
Jessy McDonald	do.		2	"		
Archibald Campbell	do.	Farmer	38	"		
Jean McNeil	do.		32	"		
Mary Campbell	do.		7	"		
Lachlan Campbell	do.		2	"		
Girzie Campbell	do.		6	"		
Finlay Murchie	do.	Farmer	45	"		
Catharine Hendry	do.		35	"		
Archd. McMurchy	do.		10	"		
Charles McMurchy	do.		5	"		
Neil McMurchy	do.		3	"		
Barbara McMurchy	do.		½	"		
Duncan McRob	do.	Taylor	26	"		
Elizabeth McMurchy	do.		8	"		
Hugh Siller	do.	Farmer	55	"		
Catharine Currie	do.		62	"		
Mary Sillar	do.		27	"		
Catharine Sillar	do.		23	"		
Gilbert McKenzie	do.	Farmer	34	"		
Margt. McKenzie	do.		27	"		
Archd. McMillan	do.	Farmer		"		
Patrick McMurchie	do.	do.	17	"		
Elizabeth Kelso	do.		50	"		
Hugh McMurchie	do.	Farmer	46	"		
Archd. McMurchie	do.	do.	21	"		
Mary McMurchie	do.		17	"		
Elizabeth McMurchie	do.		14	"		
Robert McMurchie	do.		9	"		
Neil Hendry	do.	Taylor	27	"		
Coll McAlester	do.	do.	24	"		
Mary McAlester	do.		31	"		
John McVicar	Glasgow	Taylor	36	"		
Alexander Speir	do.	Clerk	19	"		

* For High Rents & Better Encouragement.
** In the "Diana." Dugald Ruthven, for North Carolina.

John Murdoch	Kilmarnock	do.	17	Jamaica
Charles Bryce	Glasgow	do.	15	do.
Duncan Buchanan	do.	do.	18	do.
Donald Campbell	Campbeltown	do.	17	do.
Archibald Campbell	do.	do.	19	do.
James Dunn	Aberdeen	do.	20	do.
Alexr. Chappell	Renfrew	do.	20	dc.
Rod. Mathewson	Inverness	do.	18	do.
John Frazer	do.	do.	19	do.
John Kerr	do.	do.	17	do.

For High Rents & better Encouragement.

In the Jamaica. Dugald Campbell for Jamaica.

(Signed) (JO. CLERK D. Collr.
(ALEXr. CAMPBELL D. Comptr.

(Endorsed)

Port Greenock.
List of Passengers
from 8th Septemr. 1774
to 15th September 1774.

Port Kirkwall. An Account of all Persons which went from Orkney in the Ship "Marlborough" of

Whitby being George Pressick Master for Savannah in Georgia.all Indented Servants to

Messrs. Browns & Gordon.

No.	Persons Names	Ages Years.	Employments.	Whether Married or Un-married.	Former Residence.	Reasons for Emigrating.
1	John Bews	32	Labourer	Married	Stromness	Cannot get Bread in this Country.
2	Isobell Bews his Wife	30		Married		Goes with her husband.
3	James Spence	40	Farmer	Married	St.Andrews	Bad Crops, charged with high prices, cannot support his Family.
4	Mary Spence his Wife	40				goes with her husband.
5	Barbara Spence)	10				
6	James Spence)their	9				} go with their parents.
7	Helen Spence)Children.	5				
8	James Kowat	13	Servant to a Farmer.	Unmarried	St.Andrews	goes for want of proper encouragement.
9	Elisabeth Mowat	19	Ditto.	Ditto.	Shetland	goes in expectation of doing better than at home.
10	Ann Johnston	19	Ditto.	Ditto.	Stenness	Assigns no other reason than that she wants to leave this Country.
11	Ann Turnbull	23	Ditto.	Ditto.	Evie	goes to seek better encouragement than she gets in this Country.
12	John Irvine	26	Weaver	Ditto.	Stromness	cannot get Bread by his Trade.
13	Adam Corrigil	32	Farmer	Married	Evie	bad Crops & loss of Cattle.
14	Janet Corrigel his Wife	29				goes with her husband.

Name	Age	Occupation	Condition	Residence	Remarks
Katharine Corrigil) their	6				go with their parents.
Wm. Corrigil) Children	5				
Robt. Corrigil)	1				
James Wildrige	17	Servant to a Farmer.	Unmarried	Holm	goes in expectation of doing better elsewhere.
Peter Petrie	10	Ditto.	Ditto.	St.Andrew	Ditto.
John Spence	45	Sailor	Married	Kirkwall	goes in expectation of doing better as he cannot get bread here.
Thomas Brass	25	A Weaver	Unmarried	Birsay	goes for want of proper encouragement in this Country
John Mowat	16	Servant to a Farmer.	Ditto.	Deerness	does not like the encouragement in this Country.
Alexander Heddle	16	Ditto.	Ditto.	Shapinshay	Ditto.
Margaret Craigie	29	Ditto.	Ditto.	Rousay	Goes to seek a better way of living.
Barkie Harvey	16	Servant	Ditto.	Kirkwall	Ditto.
James Hanigar	35	Sailor	Ditto.	Evie	Cannot support his family in this Country.
Jean Hanigar his Spouse	25	A Servant	Married	St.Olla	goes with her husband.
Magnus Halcro	42				Cannot get bread for his Family owing to bad Crops & high prices.
Elisabeth Halcro	32				goes with her husband.
Hugh Halcro their Child	6				goes with his parents.
Thomas Guthrie	42	A Farmer	Married	Stromness	bad Crops & such high prices that he could not support his Family.
Jean Guthrie his Spouse	40				goes with her husband.
Marg't. Guthrie)	18				go with their parents.
Helen Guthrie) their	17				
Adam Guthrie) Children	14				
Thomas Guthrie)	13				
John Guthrie)	10				
Jean Guthrie)	4				
Janet Guthrie)	4 mos.				
George Brough	35	A Farmer	Married	Evie	Sustained loss by his Cattle dying & cannot support his Family.
Barbara Brough his Spouse	35				goes with her husband.

No.	Name	Occupation	Condition	Parish	Age	Remarks
42	Thomas Brough				14	} go with their parents.
43	Christian Brough				12	
44	James Brough				8	
45	Helen Brough				6	
46	John Linay	A Farmer	Married	Evie	31	} Cannot support his Family owing to bad Crops & high prices.
47	Isobel Linay his Spouse				35	goes with her husband.
48	James Linay) their				7	} go with their parents.
49	Ann Linay) Children				5	
50	William Traill	Servant to a Farmer.)	Unmarried	Deerness	15	goes because the Wages is little in this Country.
51	Thomas Louttit	A Beggar	Ditto.	Stromness	10	A Beggar.
52	John Horrie	A Farmer	Married	Stenness	36	} Cannot support his Family owing to bad Crops & high prices.
53	Jean Horry his Spouse				34	goes with her husband.
54	William Horry)their				14	} go with their parents.
55	Jean Horry)Children				12	

(Endorsed)   Port Kirkwall
An Account of all persons
which went from Orkney in the
"Marlborough" of Whitby George
Pressick Masr. for Savannah in Georgia
being all Indented Servants to
Messrs. Browns & Gordon.

September 1774.

50

(P.R.C.) (T. 47/12)

List of Passengers p. the Sally John Bruce Master

for Philadelphia.

Names.	Age.	Occupation.	Former Place of Residence.	Reasons for Emigrating.
Andrew Murray Mar.	25	Taylor	Paisley	want of Employ.
William Grierson	23	Smith	Galloway	do.
Henry Robertson) Spouse &) 2 Children)		Labourer	Loathian	Too high Rented.
Thomas Watts	21	Baker	Ballantrea	want of Employ.
Hugh Crocker	20	Labourer	Lochwinnoch	do.
David Hunter	23	Shipmaster	Ayr	to take charge of a) vessel.)
William McClure	27	Mercht.	do.	to follow his Business.
Robert Lockhart	21	Farmer	Kilbarchan	do.
George Sutherland	28	do.	Neilston	do.
Alexr. Low	19	Labourer	Kilburnie	want of Employ.
Andrew Wright	20	do.	Glasgow	do.
Alexr. Lowrie	23	do.	Monkland	do.
Thos. Naiper & Spouse		Farmer	do.	do.
William Hamilton	29	do.	Kilbride	do.
John Finneleston	23	Wright	Paisley	do.
Robert Stewart	18	Smith	Glasgow	to follow his Business.
William Drummond	25	Labourer	Renfrew	want of Employ.
Violet Grant (& 4 Children)			Kilmacolm	Going to her Husband.
Robert Childs	27	Farmer	Sutherland	too High Rented.
William Milne	19	Labourer	do.	to follow his Labour.
Alexr. Grant	22	Couper	Stirling	to follow his Trade.
Donald McLean	25	Taylor	do.	do.
John Powell	21	Mate	Greenock	to go to his Station) in a new vessel.)
John McLean	19	Sailor	do.	do.
James Turnbull	19	Labourer	Glasgow	want of Employ.
Robert Swan	21	do.	Kilmelcolm	do.
Mr. Campbell & Spouse & 4 Children & a Servt. Maid.			England	to settle in America.
Willm. Cochran	27	Mate	Greenock	to go in a new Ship.
Robert Wright	25	Tinkler	Edinburgh	to follow his Business.
William do.	23	do.	do.	do.
Margt. Simpson	17	Spinster	Craufordsdyke	to see her friends.
Margt. Wilson & 3 children		do.	Sutherland	Going to her husband.
Janet Mowat & Child		do.	do.	do. her friends.
Barbray Sheils	19	do.	Glasgow	do. her husband.

Thomas Majoribanks	25	Baker	do.	to follow his business.
Andrew Young	19	Taylor	do.	want of Employ.
James Mitchell	23	Weaver	Paisley	do.
John Galloway	25	do	do.	do.
William Christie	21	Wright	Glasgow	to follow his Business.
William Gardner	24	do.	do.	do.

The above List of Passengers from the 30th Septr. 1774

Incl. to the 7th Octr. 1774 Excl.

(Signed) (JO. CLERK D. Coll^r.
(ALEX. CALPBELL D. Com^r.

(Endorsed)

List of Emigrants from
Scotland to Philadelphia
betwn. 30 Sep^r. & 7 Octr. 1774.

R. 15 Octr. 1774. J.R.

52

(P.R.O.) (T. 47/12)

(List of Passengers from the 7th October 1774
(
Port Greenock.　(inclusive to the 14th October 1774 exclusive in
(
(the Ship "Countess" of Dumfries Robert Eason
(
(Master for Charlestown.

Names.	Occupation.	Age.	Former Residence.	Upon what account they go.
Francis Beatie	Farmer	22	Dumfries Shire	Want of Business.
William Blacklock	do.	23	do.	do.
Andrew Johnston	do.	30	do.	do.
John Cearl	do.	40	do.	do.
William Rodeak	do.	35	do.	do.
John Brown	Joiner	18	do.	do.
John Paisley	Weaver	23	do.	do.
Mrs. Paisley		26	do.	To follow her Husband.
Mrs. Cearl		50	do.	do.
John Heastie	Shoemaker	30	Perth Shire	For want of Business.
David Campbell	Taylor	30	do.	do.
James Pittegrew	Merchant	28	Glasgow	do.
Andrew Thornson	do.	20	do.	do.
Edward Corbett	do.	20	Edinburgh	do.
James Carson		12	Dumfries	do.
James Fife	Merchant	35	Renfrew Shire	do.
James Paisley	Farmer	26	Dumfries Shire	do.

(Signed)　(JO. CLERK D. Collr.
(ALEXr. CAMPBELL D. Comptr.

(Endorsed)

Port Greenock.

List of Passengers
to South Carolina
from 7th to 14th Octr. 1774.

R. 20 Octr. 1774. J.R.

(P.R.O.) (T. 47/12)

Port Kirkaldy.

(A List of Persons who have taken their
(
(Passage for Antigua on board the
(
("Jamaica Packet" Robt. Smith Master, from
(
(17th, to 23rd October 1774.

Names.	Former Residence.	Age.	Occupation.	Reason for Emigration.
John Lawson	Schetland	36	Fisherman	)
Cathn. Lawson Wife) to do.)	do.	34	(And three Children)	)) They Emigrate
James George	do.	22	Labourer	) in hopes of
Adam Lisk	do.	30	Mariner	) earning their
Margary Lisk Wife)	do.	24	and a Daughter of 9) years old.)	) Bread in a) more easy
Robert Johnstone	do.	34	Fisherman	)Manner than
Mary Johnstone Wife) to do.)	do.	30	and 5 Childn. of 14,) 11,8,7 & 3 yrs. old.)	) in their) Native
Margt. Fife	Edinburgh	21	A Spinster	) Country.
Margaret Gordon	do.	27	do.	)
William Dewar	Burnisland	30	Blacksmith	)
Jane Dewar Wife) to do.)	do.	28	(and two small Children)	)

(Signed) (ROBERT WHYT Collr.
(PHILIP PATON Comptr.

(Endorsed)

Port Kirkaldy.

List of Emigrants from the
17th to the 23rd of October 1774.

54

(P.R.O.) (T. 47/12)

Port Stornaway.   An Account of the Number of Persons who
have Emigrated to America in the Ship "Peace and Plenty" of
and for New York.   Charles McKenzie Mr.

Persons Names.	Ages.	Occupation or Employment	Former Residence.	Ports or Place to which they have gone.	*On what Account and for what purpose they have left the Country.
William McKenzie	45	Farmer	(Auch-(Main-) (hall,(land)	New York	
Mary McKenzie	44	dos. Wife	Do.		do.
Catherine McKenzie	19	dos. daughter	Do.		do.
Barbara McKenzie	16	do. do.	Do.		do.
Mally McKenzie	14	do. do.	Do.		do.
Ann McKenzie	12	do. do.	Do.		do.
Florance McKenzie	10	do. do.	Do.		do.
Thomas McKenzie	9	do. Son	Do.		do.
Murdock McKenzie	7	do. do.	Do.		do.
Bell McKenzie	3	do. daughter	Do.		do.
Nelly McKenzie	1	do. do.	Do.		do.
John Martin	42	dos. Servant	Do.		do.
Ann Cameron	21	dos. Servant	Do.		do.
Murdo Cameron	47	Tennant	Do.		do.
Mary Cameron	47	dos. Wife	Do.		do.
Bell Cameron	17	dos. daughter	Do.		do.
Jean Cameron	15	do. do.	Do.		do.
Mary Cameron	13	do. do.	Do.		do.
Ann Cameron	11	do. do.	Do.		do.
Kenneth Cameron	9	dos. Son	Do.		do.
Murdock Cameron	7	do. do.	Do.		do.
Hector Cameron	1	do. do.	do.		do.
Keneth McLenan	21	Servant	Contin, on ye) Mainland)		do.
John McLean	20	do.	Lochbroom on -do.		do.
Alexr. Cameron	30	do.	Auch:hall on -do.		do.
Murdock McKenzie	27	do.	Bly Sarry on -do.		do.
John McKenzie	17	do.	Polue on -do.		do.
William McKenzie	15	do.	do. on -do.		do.
John McKenzie	30	Taylor	Lochbroom on -do.		do.
Ann McKenzie	18	Servant	Coiduch on -do.		do.
Ann McCran	27	do.	Lochbroom on -do.		do.
Mary McCran	25	do.	do. on -do.		do.
Isabell McKenzie	17	do.	do. on -do.		do.
Murdock McLeod	32	Farmer	Coiduch on -do.		do.

* All Emigrated on Account of their being greatly reduced in their Circumstances.

Christian McLeod	30	dos. Wife	do.	do.	
May McLeod	8	dos. daughter	do.	do.	
Isabell McLeod	1	do. do.	do.	do.	
Rannald McLeod	50	Farmer	do.	do.	
Isabell Gray	25	dos. Servant	do.	do.	
John Paterson	30	Blacksmith	Stornaway	do.	
Margt. Paterson	23	dos. Wife	do.	do.	
John Paterson	1	dos. Son	do.	do.	
James Morison	14	dos. Apprentice	do.	do.	
Margt. Bain	36	dos. Servant	do.	do.	
Mary McKenzie	25	Farmers daughter) Served her Brother)	do.	do.	
Isabell McKenzie	18	do.	do.	do.	
Alexr. McKenzie	12	Merchts. Son) Schoolboy)	dc.	do.	
Neill McLeod	34	Merchant	do.	do.)	
Margt. McLeod	26	dos. Wife	do.	do.)	
John McLeod	6	dos. Son	do.	do.)	All Emigrated
Janet McLeod	4	dos. daughter	do.	do.)	on Account
Allan McLeod	2	dos. Son	do.	do.)	of the
Catherine Sutherland	38	dos. Servant	do.	do.)	Preceding
Murdoch Martin	40	Sherrief Officer	do.	do.)	Reason
John Martin	10	dos. Son	do.	do.)	
John McKenzie	20	Servant	do.	do.)	
Murdoch McKenzie	17	do.	do.	do.)	
Margt. Grahame	18	do.	do.	do.)	
Isabell Grahame	17	do.	do.	do.)	

All Emigrated on Account of their being greatly reduced in their Circumstances.

```
No. of Men       18        Custom ho  Stornaway)
No. of Women     24        14 November 1774    )
No. of Children  17
    Total No.    59        (Signed) (ARCHd. SMITH Collr.
                                    (JOHN REID compr.
```

(Endorsed)

```
Port Stornaway.
An Account of the number of
persons who have Emigrated
to America in the Ship "Peace
and Plenty"of & for New
York.  Charles McKenzie Master.
              14th Novr. 1774.
```

(P.R.O.) (T. 47/12)

Port Glasgow 30th. March 1775.

A List of Persons who have taken their Passage from
Port Glasgow for Quebec on board the Ship "Friendship"
John Smith Master.

```
John Fraser,   aged 25 Years)
James Goldie        25      )
Robert Boyd         25      )    Ships Carpenters
Hugh McHutchison    24      )    from Airshire
John Dick           24      )    going out to
David Andrew        24      )    build Vessels.
James Oliver        23      )
Andrew Valantine    13      )
```

(Signed) ARCHd. BUCHANAN T. Surveyor.

(Endorsed)

30 Mar 1775
List of Persons who
have taken their
passage from Glasgow
to Quebec.
R. 5 April 1775

(T. 47/12)

Port Greenock.

List of Passengers from this Port from the 7th Apl.

1775 to the 14th Apl. 1775 Exclusive.

Passengers Names.	Former Residence.	Occupation and Employment.	Age.	To what Port or Place Bound.	On what account and for what purpose they go.	*In what ship they take their Passage.
John Hall	Inshanan	a Farmer	46	(Salem)		
Jean Allison	Do.		39	(in North)		
William Hall	Do.	a Farmer	12	(America.)		
John Hall	do.		8	Do.)		
Jennet Hall	Do.		5	Do.)	Racking	
Robert Hall	Do.		2½	Do.)	Rents.	
James Hall	Do.		1	Do.)		
Daniel McKenzie	Dundee	a Farmer	29	Do.)		
William McKay	Do.	Do.	34	Do.)		
Helen Boyd	Do.		26	Do.)		
Helen McKay	Do.		1	Do.)		
William Tassie	Glasgow	a Smith	27	Do.)	Want of)	
Henry Buchanan	Do.	a Wright	24	Do.)	Employment.)	
Thos. McKisson	Perth	a Shoe Maker	22	Do.)	Do.	
Duncan Smith	Paisley	a Horse) Ferier)	34	Do.)	Do.	
Margaret McLean	Do.		30	Do.)		
Jean Cunningham	Stirling		26	Do.)		
Mary Dunmore	Glasgow		27	Do.)	Want of	
John Dunmore	Do.		12	Do.)	Service.	
John Watson	Do.	a Cooper	20	Do.)		
Margaret Wilson	Do.		24	Do.)		
John Wilson	Glams.	a Farmer	36	Do.)		
Peter Wilson	Do.	Do.	14	Do.)		
Robert Muir	Perth	Do.	22	Do.)	Packing	
James Dickman	Do.	Do.	26	Do.)	Rents.	
Grozel Brunton	Do.	-	25	Do.)		
James Thomson	Glasgow	a Coal) Hewer)	42	Do.	For Wealth	
Jean Buchanan	Do.		37	Do.	Do.	
William Russell	Coupar	a Farmer	24	Do.)	Racking	
Patrick White	Do.	Do.	26	Do.)	Rents.	

* In the 'Glasgow Packet." Alexr. Porterfield Master for Salem.

James Gardner)	Stirling	a Farmer	36	New York	Too high
dos. Spouse)	"		33	Do.	Rental.
& 4 children)					
Archd. McVicar)	Do.	Do.	28	Do.	Do.
Dos. Spouse)			26	Do.	
& a Daughter)					
Do. Servant Man)			21	Do.	
Danl. Gray)	Bredalbin	a Farmer	32	Do.	Do.
Dos. Spouse)			29		
& 3 children)					
John Cowan	Do.	Labourer	19	Do.	Want of employme
John Lyle)	Caithness	Farmer	27	Do.	Too high
Dos. Spouse)			25		Rental.
& 2 Children)					
William Monteath	Do.	Do.	28	Do.	Do.
Dos. Spouse			24	Do.	
David Cullens	Dundee	Labourer	21	Do.	Want of employme
David McIntosh)	Perth	Farmer	23	Do.	Too high Rent al.
Dos. Spouse)					
& Children)					
Jannet Summers)	Glasgow		32	Do.	Going t
& 4 Children)					Husband.
Jannet McFarlane	Do.	Spinster	19	Do.	Do. (
John Fisher)	Bredalbin	Farmer	45	Do.	Too high
Dos. Spouse)			41	Do.	Rental.
& 8 Children)					
Finlay Fisher)	Do.	Do.	24	Do.	Do.
Dos. Spouse)			22	Do.	
& 3 Children)					
Dond. McNaughton)	Do.	Do.	30	Do.	Do.
Dos. Spouse)			27	Do.	
& 5 Children)					
Archd. Fisher)	Do.	Do.	35	Do.	Do.
Dos. Spouse)			34	Do.	
& 5 Children)					
Donald Fisher)	Do.	Do.	26	Do.	Do.
Dos. Spouse)			22	Do.	
& 2 Children)					
Alexr. Steel	Glasgow	Labourer	27	Do.	Want of Employmen
Robt. Roxburgh	Keppen	Do.	18	Do.	Do.
Walter Anderson	Do.	Do.	29	Do.	Do.
John Elder	Glasgow	Smith	23	Do.	Do.
Isobell Fife)	Paisley		27	Do.	Going to Husband.
& a Child)					
Hugh McCallum)	Angus	Farmer	32	Do.	Too high)
Dos. Spouse)			29	Do.	Rental.)
& 4 Children)					

In the "Lilly." Thomas Cochrane Master for New York.

Name	Place	Occupation	Age	Destination	Reason
Jame ...addie)	Montrose	a Farmer	33	New York	Too High Rented.
D... ...pouse)			31		
& ...nildren)					
J... ...ogan	Paisley	Wright	19	Do.	Want of Employment.
J... ...inlay	Do.	Weaver	21	Do.	Do.
Will... ...Buchannan	Do.	Do.	25	Do.	Do.
Wal... Brock)	Glasgow	Merchant	29	Do.	To Push his Fortune.
...Spouse)			28		
...hildren)					
...ewart)	Do.		39	Do.	Going to her Husband.
...hildren)					
Mar...et Buchannan)	Do.		35	Do.	Do.
Do.)					
...Hay	Stirling	Joiner	36	Do.	Want of Employ.
...Son			15	Do.	Going with his Father.
D...Morison	Do.	Farmer	28	Do.	Too high Rented.
...an Morison			25	Do.	Going with her Brother.
...Forbes Mc)	Edinburgh	Barber	23	Do.	Want of Employ.
Kenzie.)					
...ddock	Kilmacolm	Labourer	27	Do.	Do.
Ma...McLeod)	Paisley		29	Do.	Going to her Husband.
...Children)					
...m Wallace	Do.	Weaver	36	Do.	Want of Employ.
...ingus	Forfar	Farmer	31	Do.	Too High Rented.
...Thomas	Paisley	Taylor	27	Do.	Want of Employ.
...Graham	Glasgow	Do.	23	Do.	Do.
...King	Edinburgh	Wright	25	Do.	Do.
...cLarlan	Do.	Do.	21	Do.	Do.
...Miller	Kilbarchan	Farmer	27	Do.	Too High Rented.
...Spouse			24		
...Miller)	Do.	Do.	37	Do.	Do.
...Spouse)			33		
...Children)					
...Servant Man)			25		
...McLellan	Glasgow	Labourer	27	Do.	Want of Employ.
...am Atcheson	Dumbarton	Do.	29	Do.	Do.
...Christie	Glasgow	Smith	23	Do.	Do.
...n Christie (sic)	Do.	Wright	21	Do.	Do.
...om McMartine	Do.	Cooper	29	Do.	Do.
...n McMartine	Do.	Taylor	25	Do.	Do.
...McMartine	Do.	Brush) Maker)	23	Do.	Do.
...ian Robinson	Kilenbrie	Farmer	37	Do.	Too High Rented.
...ald Robinson	Do.	Do.	32	Do.	Do.
...liam Simpson	Lochwinnoch	Labourer	31	Do.	Want of Employ.
W...liam Marshall	Renfrew	Do.	27	Do.	Do.
...rt Marshall	Glasgow	Wright	29	Do.	Do.
...ge Garland	Do.	Barber	25	Do.	Do.
A...ew Leckie	Anderston	Labourer	19	Do.	Do.
William McLea	Islay	Do.	29	Do.	Do.

In the "Lilly." Thomas Cochrane Master for New York.

William Mitchell	Paisley	Do.	32	New York	Do.
Alexr. Thomson	Stirling	Wright	23	Do.	Do.
James McEwen	Do.	Nailer	19	Do.	Do.
David Musket)	Do.	Farmer	38	Do.	Too high Rental.
& 2 Sons)					
Jannet Ferguson	Paisley		32	Do.	Going to her Husband.
Margaret Summers	Do.		27	Do.	Do.
William Paterson	Glasgow	Copper)	29	Do.	Want of Employ.
		Smith)			
William Robinson	Paisley	Smith	25	Do.	Do.
William Dodds	Lanark	Labourer	29	Do.	Do.
William Baird	Lithgow	Do.	23	Do.	Do.
James Paul	Air	Do.	27	Do.	Do.
Hugh Lariman	Do.	Do.	22	Do.	Do.
John Walker	Paisley	Shoemaker	25	Do.	Do.
William Gibson	Do.	Weaver	27	Do.	Do.
Dos. Spouse					
Jean Stewart)			22	Do.	Going to her Husband.
& 2 Children)					
Rabina Eaton)			25	Do.	Do.
& a Child)					
Isobell Malcolm			21	Do.	Going to her Friends.
John Chalmers	Parlick	Labourer	25	Do.	)
Andrew Dickson	Edinburgh	Do.	29	Do.	)
Francis McKenzie	Islay	Do.	29	Do.	)
James Duncan	Falkirk	Do.	15	Do.	)
John McCallum	Stornway	Do.	19	Do.	)
Ann Grieve	Edinburgh		17	Do.	)
David McLaurence	Do.	Barber	23	Do.	)
David Lyle	Do.	Labourer	29	Do.	) All Indented
Mary Smith	Do.		25	Do.	) for Want
Robert Mathieson	Elgin	Do.	23	Do.	) of Employ.
William Gilmour	Edinburgh	Book)	27	Do.	)
		Binder)			)
Margaret Jackson	Do.		21	Do.	)
Eustian(?)Mathieson	Do.		17	Do.	)
Peggy McLean	Do.		19	Do.	)
Jannet Lament	Do.		18	Do.	)
Jannet Ruddiman	Montrose		20	Do.	)
John McMillan	Wigton	Labourer	25	Do.	)
Thomas Inglish	Kilmarnock	Do.	19	Do.	)
Fanny Ramsay	Edinburgh		23	Do.	)

In the "Lilly." Thomas Cochrane Master for New York.

JOHN DUNLOP T.S.
ED. PENMAN D. Collr.

JOHN McVICAR D. Compr.

P.T.O.

(P.R.O.) (T. 47/12)

Port Greenock.

List of Passengers from the 28th April 1775

Incl. to the 5 May 1775 Exclusive.

Names	Age.	Occupation.	Former Place of Residence.	Reasons for Emigration.
Rob. McFarlane)& 5	45	Farmer	Keathness	Too high Rental.
dos. Spouse)Children	40			do.
Tho. Paton	29	Shoemaker	Edinburgh	Want of Employ.
Thomas Small	32	Smith	Glasgow	do.
James Low	25	Weaver	do.	do.
Thos. Dick	28	Wright	Stirling	do.
Willm. Cunningham	35	Farmer	Dumblain	Too high Rental.
John McLean	35	Labourer	Lochaber	Want of employ.
Duncan McLean	31	do.	do.	do.
William Herriot	22	Baker	Gorbals	do.
Thos. Barcklay	29	Farmer	Stewartton	Too high Rental.
Jas. Barcklay	25	do.	do.	do.
James Anderson	27	Wright	Alloa	To follow his) trade.)
John Anderson	25	do.	do.	do.
Margaret Anderson	21			)going with
Jannet Anderson	18			)their brothers.
Hugh Wait	27	Farmer	Neilston	Too high Rental.
John Black	25	do.	Kilsyth	do.
Duncan Ferguson	36	do.	Falkirk	do.
dos. Spouse	35			
Wm. Reia	29	Barber	Paisley	Want of Employ.
Andrew Massie	32	Taylor	Glasgow	do.
Alexr. Donald	37	Labourer	Killcarn	do.
Robt. McGlashan)& 2	39	Farmer	Stranrar	Too high Rental.
dos. Spouse)Children	37			
Willm. Alexander	25	Shoemaker	Dumfarline	Want of Employ.
John McAlester	30	Coppersmith	Edinburgh	dc.
John Mearson	31	Wright	Stirling	do.
Joseph McDonald	27	Labourer	Wigtown)	
Archd. Buchannan	35	Pewterer	Edinr.)	Indented for)
Jean McGlashan	14		Stranrar.)	Want of Employ.)
Cathrine McGlashan	11		do.)	
Robert McCallachy	29	Watchmaker	Dundee	do.
David Howie)& 3	38	Farmer	Sutherland	Too high Rental.
dos. Spouse)Children	35			
Peter McGibbon	27	Taylor	Paisley	Want of Employ.

P. the "Christy" Hugh Rellie Master for New York & Georgia.

Mathw. Lyon	49	Weaver)		do.
Mary Lyon his Spouse	50	)		
James Lyon	21	Weaver)	Glasgow	do.
John Kennburgh	24	Labourer)		do.
James Kennburgh	27	do.)		do.
John McNabb	24	do.)		do.
Jean Campbell his)	19	)	Argyleshire	
Spouse)		)		
Tibby McNabb	20	To get a)) husband.))		
Dougs. McVey	30	Labourer	do.	Want of Employ.
James Buges	27	Merchant	Edinr.	to follow his) business.)
Margt. Hog his Spouse	25	to comfort) her husband)	do.	

P. The Ulysses Jas. Wilson Master for No. Carolina.

ED. PENMAN D. Collr.
JOHN McVICAR D. Compr.

(Endorsed)

Port Greenock.
List of Passengers
from 28th April 1775
to the 5th May 1775.

List of Emigrants shipped (sic) on Board

Carsthorn 1st May 1775. the "Lovely Felly" of Whavon, Wm. Shiridan

Master for St. Johns Island North America.

Emigrants Names.	Ages.	Occupa-tions.	Place of Residence.	County.	Quality.	For what Reasons they Leave Scotland.
1 Thomas Henderson	32	Joiner	Hoddham	Annadale	Countryman	(To seek) (better) (bread) (than he) (can get) (here.)
2 Margery Hogg Wife	32				do.	
3 Martha his Daughter	8				do.	
4 Hanny do.	4				do.	
5 Thomas his son	1				do.	
6 Joseph Graive	36	Weaver	Newabby	Galloway	Countryman	(The same) (reason as) (above.)
7 Marrion Buckley We.	34				do.	
8 John his son	10				do.	
9 Robert do.	8				do.	
10 Mary his daughter	3				do.	
11 Joseph Clark	45	Joiner	Sanquhar	Nithsdale	Countryman	(To get) (better) (bread.)
12 Ann Wilkie Wife	36				do.	
13 Ann Clark Daughter	4				do.	
14 Joseph his son 15 months					do.	
15 Robert Braiden	38	Labourer	Dumfries	Nithsdale	Countryman	(To pro-) (vide for) (his fam-) (ily a) (better) (liveli-) (hood.)
16 Jean Kirkpatrick We.	26				do.	
17 James his son	7				do.	

18 William	do.	4)Twines			do.		
19 David	do.	4)			do.		
20 Edward	do.	Moths.7			do.		

21 William Clark	30	Gardener	Carlowrock	do.	do.	do.
22 Grizoe Kissock Wife	30					
23 John Clark Child	10) months)					

24 William Graham	25	Labourer	Drysdale	do.	do.	do.
25 Jannet Rogerson	25					
26 James McCullock	48	Labourer	Dumfries	do.		
27 Jannet Johnston	60					

28 John Aitken	50	Labourer	Carlowrock	do	do.	do.
29 Margaret Lowden We.	36					
30 James his son	17					
31 Goddion do.	7					
32 Margaret his Daughr	4					
33 Agnews do.	2					

34 James Douglas	57	Labourer	Newabby	Galloway	do.	To mend) Himself.)
35 Jannet Neish	53					
36 James his son	8					

(sic)

37 Anthony Culton	30	Labourer	Traquhar	do.	do.	do.
38 Jannet McCaughter	36					
39 Marrion his daur.	12					
40 Grizel do.	7					
41 Jannet do.	5					
42 Ann do. moths.7						
43 Robert his son	10					
44 John do.	4					

45 William Douglas	21	Labourer	Kirkboan	Galloway	Countryman
46 John Douglas	25	do.	do.		

47 James Gibson	45	Chapman	do.	do.
48 Adam Gibson	31	Labourer	do.	do.

49 David Irvine	37	Labourer	St. Mungo	Anandale	Countryman
50 Margaret Graham	37				
51 William his son	11				
52 Jean A Daughter	7				
53 James a son	3				

54	Robert Marshall	33	Weaver	Farquhar	Galloway	Countryman	To get a) better Em-) ployment.)
55	Elizabeth do.	32					
56	John his son	8					
57	Andrew do.	4					
58	Jamer do.	Ms. 4					

59	Andrew Brigg	30	Black-) smith)	Kirkboam	Galloway	Countryman	To mend) his) Fortune.)
60	Margaret Griver	28				do.	

61	John Carson	20	Labourer	Colvend	do.	Countryman	To better) himself.)
62	Charles Carson	18	do.	do.	do.	do.	do.

63	Gavin Johnson	22	School-) master)	Bothwell	Lanark	Scholar	To get a) place.)
64	William Blair	30	Mariner	Colvend	Galloway		For his) health.)
65	Charles Aikin	22	Clerk	do.	do.		To look) after the) others.)
66	Thomas Chrisholm	36	Farmer	Kirkboan	do.		do.

These are (to) Certify that the above Number of Sixty Six persons I
have examined as above written by me Willm. Graive.

List of Families and Persons Names received from Mr. Sheriden
which is to embark at different places as under.   Viz.

1 Thomas Trumbell	)		Run away)
	)		from this)
	)	to be shipped at Douglas Isleman	place.)
2 Jean Mackay his Wife	)		
3)Trumbells 3 Children.	)		
4)			
5)			

6 Robert Douglas	)	to be shipped at Whitehaven	Run away.
7 John Grinlaw	)		do.

8 Anthony McClilan)
)   A man of)

                                           good)

```
8 Anthony McClilan   )                                          A man of  )
                     )                                          good      )
                     )To be shipped at Ballcarry Port Kirkcud-) character.)
9)                   )                           bright.)
10)                  )
11)McClilans 5 children)
12)
13)
```
_____

```
14 John McClean)                                    Good character.
15 His Wife    ) To be shipped at do. Port Kirkcudbright.
16 His Son
```
_____

(<u>Endorsed</u>)

Acct. of Passengers from
Dumfries to America.

Port Leith. An Account of Passengers and Servants on board
the "Friendship" Thomas Jann Master from Leith to Philadelphia.

Names	Ages.	Former Residence.	Occupation.	Whither Bound.	Reason for Leaving the Country.
Thomas Breymer	15	Dundee	Groom Boy	Philadelphia	Want of Employ-) ment.)
William Laing	15	Paisley	Weaver	do.	do.
William Shirmlaw	14	Glasgow	Nothing	do.	do.
David Dunbar	14	Wick	do.	do.	do.
Thomas Balantine	17	Dundee	Weaver	do.	do.
David Panton	19	Rattray	Taylor	do.	To better his) Fortune.)
John McKay	15	Rogert	Ballard seller	do.	To prosecute) his Calling.)
Mary Morrison	20	London	Milliner	do.	do.
Adam Gordon	18	Aberdeen	Farmer	do.	do.
James Mackay	16	Edinburgh	Nothing	do	Want of Employ-) ment.)
Thomas Pitterkin	20	St.Augustus	do.	do.	do.
James Duncan	16	Howthorndean	Storekeeper	do.	do.
John Ormond	16	Angus	Labourer	do.	do.
George Mitchell	18	Glasgow	Joiner	do.	do.
Margaret Seton	22	Aberdean	Servant	do.	do.
Jean Simpson	20	Dunbar	do.	do.	do.
Christian King	18	Perth	do.	do.	do.
Cathrine Dick	21	Breton	do.	do.	do.
Jannet Muir	29	Edinburgh	do.	do.	do.
Ann Muir	20	do.	do.	do.	do.
Kenneth McKenzie	25	do.	Gardener	do.	do.
Alexander Sands	17	do.	Chapman	do.	
John Middleton	15	do.	Nothing	do.	Push his fortune.
Jean Smith	21	Dumfirnline	Sergeant	do.	do.
Charles McIntire	14	Kilryth	do.	do.	do.
Margaret Philip	18	Edinburgh	do.	do.	do.
Mary Clark	23	Aberdeen	Servant	do.	Better their) fortune.)
Janet Stevenson	20	do.	do.	do.	do.
Ann Urquhart	17	Ross	do.	do.	do.
Betty Lockhart	15	Foubriggs	db.	do.	do.
Emelia McLead (sic)	18	Inverness	do.	do.	do.
Barbara Campbell	18	Ross	do.	do.	do.
Margaret McRae	19	Edinburgh	do.	do.	do.
John Cassels	15	do.	do.	do.	do.
Robert Small	16	Perth	Barber	do.	do.

John Lesslie	15	Sutherland	Servant	do.	do.
Lucy Ross	21	Caithness	do.	do.	do.
Mary Martin	16	Edinburgh	Servant	do.	Better their Fortune.
Janet Lockhart	16	do.	do.	do.	do.
Helen Robertson	16	do.	do.	do.	do.
Mary McDonald	17	Perth	do.	do.	do.
Isobel Cassels	19	Edinburgh	do.	do.	do.
Dorothy Smith	17	Yorkshire	do.	do.	do.
Hannah Blackton	21	Edinburgh	do.	do.	do.
William Saunders	17	Angus	Ploughman	do.	do.
Andrew Barr	20	Dalkeith	Gardener	do.	do.
Daniel Robertson	18	Perth	Weaver	do.	Want of Employment.
Lewis Smith	24	Aberdeen	Silversmith	do.	Better their Fortune
James Hay	17	Edinburgh	Joiner	do.	do.
Mary Oman	21	do.	Milliner	do.	do.
Jenny Campbell	16	do.	Servant	do.	do.
Mary Cuthbert	19	do.	do.	do.	do.
Elizabeth Young	20	do.	do.	do.	do.
Isobel McKay	23	Ross	Servant	do.	do.
Kathrine McPherson	22	Inverness	do.	do.	do.
Elizabeth Fraser	20	Ross	do.	do.	do.
Isobel McKenzie	17	do.	do.	do.	do.
Elizabeth Miller	23	Perth	do.	do.	do.
B. Learmonth	21	Raths	do.	do.	dc.
Janet Balfour	18	Edinburgh	do.	do.	do.
Euph Learmonth	23	Raths	do.	do.	do.
Nelly Ross	22	Cullen	do.	do.	do.
Marget Forfar	19	Perthshire	do.	do.	do.
Charles Doig	21	do.	Weaver	do.	do.
Alexr. Dempster	18		Gardener	do.	do.
Marget Simpson	23	Dumfermline	Servant	do.	do.
Ross Steel	21	Herriot	do.	do.	do.
Isobel Arthur	27	Edinburgh	do.	do.	do.
Helen Arthur	22	do.	do.	do.	do.
Ann Craig	19	Anstruther	do.	do.	do.
Ann Steenson	19	Dysart	do.	do.	do.
Baby Abercromby	22	do.	do.	do.	do.
William Butter	30	Perth	Coppersmith	do.	Better their Fortune
Daniel Thomson	14	Forfar	Nothing	do.	do.
Janet Bruce	18	Edinburgh	Sergeant(sic)	do.	do.
Ann Bruce	16	do.	do.	do.	do.
Kat. McFarlane	17	do.	do.	do.	do.
Mary McDonald	15	Perth	do.	do.	do.
Helen Blackie(?)	25	Gifford	do.	do.	do.
Cathrine Cant	19	Edinburgh	do.	do.	do.
Mary Reid	17	do.	do.	do.	do.
Betty Oman	16	Newcastle	do.	do.	do.
Daniel Oman	15	Leith	Servant	do.	do.
James Yoiman	16	Dundee	Barber	do.	do.
Isobel Knex	21	Stirling	Servant	do.	do.
Lilly Dempster	16	Edinburgh	do.	do.	do.
Peggy Graham	21	Caithness	do.	do.	do.

Elizabeth Wyht	21	Amotmill	do.	do.	do.
Katn. Inness	20	Caithness	do.	do.	do.
John Cairns	24	Fife	Wright	do.	do.
John Lawrie	28	Kinross	Servant	do.	do.
Mary Donaldson	17	Alloa	do.	do.	do.
Peggy McPherson	17	Aberdeen	Passenger	do.	To see her friends.
Jenny Grieg	24	Edinburgh	do.	do.	do.
James Berry	18	Qr. ferry	Clockmaker	do.	Push his Fortune.
John Moodie	18	Perth	Servant	do.	do.
David Pride	18	Fife	Shoemaker	do.	do.
Alexr. Douglas	52	Perth	Labourer	do.	do.

Customhouse Leith 9th May 1775.

Signed   (DAVID DOIG, Landwaiter.
            (JAMES DAIN, Tidesman.

(Endorsed)

Acct. of Passengers from
Leith to Philadelphia.

T. 47/12.

LIST OF PASSENGERS from the 26th May 1775 Inclusive,

to 2nd June 1775 Exclusive.

Names.	From Whence.	Age.	Occupation.	On what account and for what purpose they go.	To what Place Bound.	In what Ship they take their Passage.
William Fortune	Edinburgh	50	Sadler	To better) his Fortune.)	New York	
Alexr. Hendry	do.	30	do.	do.	do.	
John McAllan	Lorn	40	Farmer	do.	do.	
Janet McAllan	do.	40	. . .	following) her husband.)	do.	
Janet do.	do.	20	Spinster	do. her) parents.)	do.	
Donald do.	do.	19	Farmer	do. his) do.)	do.	
Annie do.	do.	14.	Spinster	do. her) do.)	do.	
Katherine do.	do.	13	do.	do. her) do.)	do.	
James Cameron	Blair Athol	22	Farmer	to better) his Fortune.)	do.	
James Stewart	do.	21	do.	do.	do.	In the
James Ferguson.	do.	20	do.	do.	do.	Monimia
Andrew Young	Sterling	40	do.	do.	do.	Edward
Mary Young	do.	36	do.	following) her husband.)	do.	Morrison
James do.	do.	18	do.	do. parents.)	do.	Master.
Katherine do.	do.	16	do.	do.	do.	
John do.	do.	9	do.	do.	do.	
William do.	do.	4	do.	do.	do.	
Mary Ockman (sic)	do.	36	Spinster	following) her Husband.)	do.	
Margaret do.	do.	16	do.	do. parents.)	do.	
Nelly do.	do.	9	do.	do.	do.	
Lise do.	do.	5	. . . .	do.	do.	
William Bald	Glasgow	30	Wright	To better) his Fortune.)	do.	
May do.	do.	24	. . .	following) her Husband.)	do.	
Mary do.	do.	3		her) parents.)	do.	

Thomas Robeson	Sterling	40	Farmer	to buy land.	New York
May do.	do.	36	Spinster	following)	do.
			(sic)	her Husband.)	
May do.	do.	25	do.	do.)	do.
				her parents.)	
Agness do.	do.	20	do.	do. do.	do.
Alexander do.	do.	16	Farmer	his do.	do.
James do.	do.	11	. . .	do. do.	do.
Betty do.	do.	9	Spinster	do. her do.	do.
Thomas Buchan.	do.	30	Farmer	do. his)	do.
				master.)	
Robert Bain	do.	30	Wright	want of Em-)	do.
				ployment.)	
Alexr. Hutchon	do.	25	do.	do. do.	do.
John Ogilvie	do.	30	do.	do. do.	do.
Alexr. Thomson	do.	30	do.	do. do.	do.
James Cameron	do.	25	do.	do. do.	do.
Jannet Cameron	do.	21	. . . .	following)	do.
				her Husband.)	
Donald McPherson	do.	32	Farmer)		do.
Jannet McTogart.	dc.	26	Wife)& four children.		do.
Duncan McPherson	Stirling	32	Farmer)		do.
Jane McBride	do.	20	Wife) 2 Children.		do.
Duncan McBride	do.	46	Farmer) 4 Sons &)		do.
Marrion Donaldson	do.	42	Wife) 5 daughters.)		do.
James Blockie	do.	45	Farmer) 3 Sons &)		do. In the
Margaret Davie	do.	41	Wife) 2 daughters.)		do. Monimia
John McDonald	do.	38	Farmer)		do. Edward
Margaret Grieve	do.	42	Wife) 3 daughters.		do. Morrison
Marrion Grieve	Down	35	Seamstress to push her)		do Master.
			Fortune.)		
Katherine Brown	do.	32	do. do.		do.
Robert Adam	Sterling	16	. . . .		do.
Colin Campbell	Perthshire	24	Gentleman to be a)		do.
			Merchant.)		
Robert Brodie	do.	37	Wright)		do.
Katty Black.	do.	27	Wife) 6 children.		do.
Donald McPherson	do.	47	Farmer) 4 Sons &)		do.
Mary McFee	do.	43	Wife) 2 daughters.)		do.
Thomas Forster	do.	36	Shoemaker)		do.
Jannet Tasie	. . . .	38	Wife) 3 daughters.		do.
George Robson	do.	49	Taylor) 6 Sons &)		do.
Marrion Weir	do.	46	Wife) 1 daughter)		do.
George Blackburn.	do.	32	Mason		do.
Peter More	do.	31	do.		do.
Patrick Douglas	do.	35	do.		do.
Duncan Munro	do.	43	Taylor)		do.
Jannet Brown	do.	40	Wife) 4 Sons.		do.
James Campbell	do.	41	Farmer)		do.
Jane Campbell	do.	36	Wife) 3 Children		do.
Dugald Grigerson	do.	32	Farmer		do.

Name	Place	Age	Occupation	Destination / Notes
Jane Blue	Perthshire	30	Wife	New York
Peter Macintosh	Glasgow	28	Wright	
Peter McKinlay	do.	24	do.	
George Munro	do.	30	do.	
Thos. Macintosh	do.	26	Mason	
John Hart	do.	32	do.	
Donald McFaideb	Perthshire	42	Farmer	
Ronald Campbell	do.	36	do.	
Duncan Campbell	do.	25	do.	
Sarah Campbell	do. Maid	21	Servant with the master.	
James Campbell	do.	36	Farmer	In the
Hugh Campbell	do.	45	Labourer	Monimia
Hary Burnside	do.	40	do.)	Edward
Margart. Burnside	do.	38	Wife.) & 7 children.	Morrison
Hugh Lockhead	do.	39	Farmer)	Master.
Isobell Bruce	do.	42	Wife) & 5 children.	
Hugh Black	do.	42	Farmer)	
Jannet Brown	do.	38	Wife) & 3 children.	
James Bruce	do.	48	Farmer)	
Janet Black	do.	44	Wife) 10 children.	
Duncan McIntire	do.	42	Mason	
Donald Roy	Glasgow	25	Taylor	
Robert Curry	Kelsyth	26	Weaver	
Peter Brown	Glasgow	23	Barber	
Robert Brownlie	Perthshire	36	Labourer	
John Henderson	Lasswood	26	Gentleman	

The above gives almost all the same Reasons for Emigrating
Viz. Want of Employment, High Rents and hopes of better
their Fortune.

Name	Place	Age	Occupation	Destination / Notes
Walter McFarlane	-	20	Gentleman. To be a) Merchant.) North	In the "Ajax," Robert
Mary Menzies	-	25	Lady Going to) Caro- her husband.) lina.	Cunningham Master.

(EDWARD PELMAN D. Collector.
Signed. (JOHN McVICAR D. Compr.
(JOHN DUNLOP Tide Surveyor.

T. 47/12.)

Port Stranraer.   An Account of Emigrants Shipped at

Stranraer the 31st May 1775 on board the Jackie of Glasgow

James Morris Master for New York in North America, with a

description of their Age, Quality, Occupation, Employment,

Former Residence, On what Account and for what purposes

they leave the Country.

No.	Emigrants Names.	Ages Years.	Occupation or Employment.	Former Residence.	To what Port or Place Bound.	On what Account and for what purposes they leave the Country.
1	John Adair	45	Labourer	Beak	New York	In hopes of) making Rich.)
2	Janet McNillie	43		do.	do.	
3	Janet Adair	17		do.	do.	
4	Jean Adair	14		do.	do.	
5	Agnes Adair	10		do.	do.	
6	John Adair	6		do.	do.	
7	Alexr. Adair	4		do.	do.	
8	Janet Milwain	58		New Luce	do.	To See 2 Sons.
9	Sarah McMiken	21		do.	do.	
10	Janet McMiken	36		do.	do.	
11	Thos. Cooper	4		do.	do.	
12	Jas. Cooper	3		do.	do.	
13	Jas. Hunter	29	House Wright	Kirmachel	do.	In hopes of good) Employment.)
14	Janet McKinnel	22		do.	do.	
15	John Hunter	5 months.		do.	do.	
16	Janet McWilliam	60		do.	do.	With her Son.
17	Mary McKinnel	25		do.	do.	For a better way) of doing.)
18	Robt. Maxwell	50	Weaver	Inch	do.	In hopes of good) employment.)
19	Martha Carnochan	50		do.	do.	
20	Margt. Maxwell	24		do.	do.	
21	Janet Maxwell	20		do.	do.	
22	Sarah Maxwell	17		do.	do.	
23	Martha Maxwell	11		do.	do.	
24	Jas. McCracken	28	Taylor	Stonykirk	do.	In hopes of good) Employment.)
25	Jas. Matheson	38	Labourer	New Luce	North) Carolina)	do.
26	Jean McQuiston	27		do.	do.	

74

(Account continued.)

No.	Name	Age	Occupation	Parish	Destination	Reason
27	Margt. Matheson	4		New Luce	North Carolina)	
28	Jno. McQuiston	46	Labourer	Inch	do.	In hopes of better) Employment.)
29	Cathr. Walker			New Luce	do.	For a better way) of living.)
30	John Main	36	Labourer	Glenluce	New York	In hopes of better) Employment.)
31	Margt. Torborn	36		do.	do.	
32	Anne Main	5		Glenluce	New York	
33	John Main	3		do.	do.	
34	Alexr. McMiken	20	Labourer	Inch	do.	He did not choose) to stay at home.)
35	John Craig	20	Weaver	Stonykirk	do.	In hopes of better) business.)
36	Jas. McBride	38	Farmer	New Luce	North Carolina)	The High Rent of) Land.)
37	Janet McMiken	39		do.	do.	
38	Archd. McBride	7		do.	do.	
39	Eliz. McBride	5		do.	do.	
40	Jenny McBride	4		do.	do.	
41	Geo. McKie	48	Farmer	Inch	New York	In hopes of better) bread.)
42	Jean McMiken	48		do.	do.	
43	Peter McKie	16	Weaver	do.	do.	
44	To. McKie	14		do.	do.	
45	Janet McKie	11		do.	do.	
46	David McKie	10		do.	do.	
47	Jean McKie	6		do.	do.	
48	Alexr. McKie	4		do.	do.	
49	Jno. Sloan	40	Weaver	do.	do.	In hopes of better) Employment.
50	Eliza. McCubbin	42		do.	do.	
51	Grizel Sloan	11		do.	do.	
52	Alexr. Sloan	10		do.	do.	
53	Jno. Sloan	8		do.	do.	
54	Jean Sloan	5		do.	do.	
55	Gilbt. McMiken	40	Labourer	do.	do.	In hopes of better) Employment.)
56	Jean McKinnel	30		do.	do.	
57	Jno. Stuart	28	Labourer	Leswalt	do.	In hopes of a better way of doing.
58	Jean McWhinie	30		do.	do.	
59	Mary Stuart	4		do.	do.	
60	Margt. Stuart	6 months		do.	do.	
61	Jas. Steven	27	Farmer	Inch	North Carolina)	In hopes of better) bread.)
62	Chrn. Steven	23		do.	do.	With her Brother.
63	Sarah Steven	16		do.	do.	do.
64	Thos. Steven	11		do.	do.	do.

(Account continued.)

65	Jno. Dalrymple	49	Farmer	New Luce	North)	The High Rent)
					Carolina)	of Land.)
66	Margt. Gordon	39		do.	do.	
67	Mary Dalrymple	19		do.	do.	
68	Jno. Dalrymple	17		do.	do.	
69	Archd. Dalrymple	15		do.	do.	
70	Jas. Dalrymple	11		do.	do.	
71	Ann Dalrymple	9		do.	do.	
72	Janet Dalrymple	7		do.	do.	
73	Jean Dalrymple	5		do.	do.	
74	Wm. Dalrymple	2		do.	do.	
75	Alexr. McBride	22	Labourer	do.	do.	In hopes of)
						better Employment.)
76	Jas. Davidson	20	Sailor	Kirkcolm	New York	In hopes of)
						making rich.)
77	Jean Davidson	22		do.	do.	With her Brother.
78	John Duff	20	A Herdsman	New Luce	North)	In hopes of)
					Carolina)	good Employment.)
79	Wm. Eckles	40	Shoemaker	Inch	do.	In Hopes of)
						good Business.)
80	Martha McKenzie	45		do.	do.	
81	John Eckles	12		do.	do.	

Customho. Stranraer 5. June 1775.

N.S.   As all the Married Women follow their Husbands and the
Children their Parents, We have inserted no Reason for
their leaving the Country, after their Names.

JOHN CLUGSTON Collr.
PATK. McINTIRE Comp.

(Endorsed)   Port Stranraer

An Account of Emigrants
Shipped at Stranraer the 31st
May 1775 on Board the "Jackie "
of Glasgow James Morris Master
for New York in North America,
with a Description of their Age,
Quality, Occupation, Employment,
former Residence, On what Account
and for what Purposes they
leave the Country.

P.T.O.

Port Kirkaldy. An Account of Emigration from this
Port and precinct to America or other Foreign ports
from the 5th of June 1775 to the 11th do. both inclusive.

Emigrants on board the Jamaica Packet of Burntisland
Thomas Smith master for Brunswick North Carolina.

Miss Elizabeth Mills & her servant going to reside
in So. Carolina from Dundee.

John Drummond & John Marshall Coopers from Leith,
goes out because they get (?) Wages than in their own
Country.

John Douglas Labourer from Dundee, goes out for the
above Occasion. John Mills and Thomas Hill Joiners
from Do. go to settled(sic) in So. Carolina.

Andrews Williamson, James Jamaison & William Mitchell,
Farmers & Fishermen from Schelland(sic) with their Wives
& Seven Children.

Farmers and Fishermen go abroad because the Land-
holders in Schetland have raised their rents so high
that they could not live without sinking the little
matter they had left(sic).   Total 20 Passengers.

N.B. no other Emigration from this Port or precinct in
the Course of this Week.

Signed (ROBERT WHYT Coll^r.
        (PHILIP PATON comp^r.

(Endorsed)

Emigrants on board
the Jamaica Packet
Thomas Smith M^r.
for Brunswick. N.
Carolina.

(P.R.O.) (T. 47/12)

Port Greenock List of Passengers from this Port from the

9. June 1775 Incl: to the 16. June 1775 Exclusive per the

"Brigantine Commerce," John Mathie Master for New York.

Names.	Age. Years.	Former Residence.	Employment.	Reasons for Emigrating.
		(Broad Albion		
Duncan Littlejohn	38	(Perthshire.	Wright	Want of Business.
Malcolm McIsaac	29	"	Smith	"
David Allen	24	"	Wright	"
Janet Stewart	19	"	Wife	"
Angers Cameron	47	"	Farmer	Over Rented.
Kathn. McDonald	32	"	Wife	"
Mary Cameron	16	"	Child	"
John Cameron	14	"	"	"
Alex. Cameron	13	"	"	"
Duncan Cameron	11	"	"	"
Alexr. Thomson	48	"	Farmer	"
Janet Korest	33	"	Wife	"
Mary McKorest	18	"	Servant	Poverty.
William Thomson	14	"	Child	"
Kathn. Thomson	11	"	"	"
Betty Thomson	9	"	"	"
Henry Thomson	1	"	"	"
James Ferguson	32	"	Wright	Poor living.
Jean McGrigor	29	"	Wife	"
Mary Ferguson	21	"	Child	"
Robert Ferguson	13	"	"	"
Helen Ferguson	11	"	"	"
Ann Ferguson	7	"	"	"
Duncan McArthur	52	"	Farmer	High Rents.
Eliza. McEwen	47	"	Wife	"
John McArthur	20	"	Mason	Want of Business.
Donald McArthur	15	"	Taylor	"
Peter McArthur	12	"	Child	"
John McArthur	11	"	"	"
Donald McArthur	2	"	"	"
William Murray	44	"	Farmer	High Rents.
Margt. McDougald	41	"	Wife	"
John Murray	22	"	Mason	Want of Business.
Alexander Murray	18	"	Taylor	"
Archd. Murray	17	"	Shoemaker	"
Christian Murray	12	"	Child	"
Kathn. Murray	8	"	"	"
James Murray	1	"	"	"

(Donald)

Names.	Age Years.	Former Residence.	Employment.	Reasons for Emigration.
Donald, McIntire	43.	(Broad Albion (Perthshire.	Schoolmaster	(Fervent zeal to (propogate Christian
Ann Walker	36	"	Wife	(knowledge.
Kathn. McIntyre	19	"	Servant	Poverty.
Ann McIntyre	17	"	"	"
Archd. McIntyre	8	"	Child	"
Eliza. Walker	18	"	Servant	"
Alexander Kay	26	"	Piper	Want of Business.
David Walker	18	"	"	"
Donald Walker	13	"	Taylor	"
Hugh McLeran	34	"	Farmer	High Rents.
John McNaughton	38	"	"	"
Jannet Anderson	30	"	Wife	Poverty.
Christn. McNaughton	14	"	Child	"
Kathn. McNaughton	11	"	"	"
Duncan McNaughton	7	"	"	"
Isobell Matlock	18	"	Servant	"
Kathn. McNaughton	3	"	Child	"
John McNaughton	3	"	"	"
Eliza. McNaughton	2	"	"	"
Daniel McNaughton	1	"	"	"
Janet McNaughton	1	"	"	"
Angus McNaughton	½	"	"	"
Peter McNaughton	½	"	"	"
Patrick Cromery	23	"	Wright	Want of Business.
James Cromery	28	"	Shoemaker	"
James McLeran	32	"	Taylor	"
Dond. McArther	59	"	Farmer	Oppression.
Kathn. McNaughton	46	"	Wife	"
John McArther	22	"	Mason	Want of Business.
Donald McArther	17	"	Taylor	"
Kathn. McArther	14	"	Child	"
Archd. McArther	8	"	"	"
James, Dun	29	"	Farmer	High Rents.
Kathn. Dun	30	"	Wife	"
John Dun	26	"	Tidler	Want of bread.
Duncan McArther	20	"	Weaver	Want of business.
Mary McDiarmed	21	"	Servant	Want of Employment.
Eliza. McDiarmed	17	"	"	"
Kathn. McDiarmed	14	"	Child	"
John McDiarmed	3	"	"	"
Jean McDiarmed	3	"	"	"
Donald McVian	39	"	Farmer	High Rents.
Duncan McVian	6	"	Child	"
John McVian	21	"	Wright	Curiosity.
Janet McNaughton	33	"	Wife	"
John McNaughton	24	"	Farmer	"
Angus Kennedy	26	"	"	"
Sarrah McVian	17	"	Servant	Want of employment.

(Peter)

Names.	Age. Years.	Former Residence.	Employment.	Reasons for Emigrating.
		(Broad Albion		
Peter McVurah	19	(Perthshire.	Founder	Want of employment.
Colin Campbell	27	"	Smith	"
Peter McMartine	21	"	"	"
Chrisn. McNaughton	20	"	Servant	"
Mary McVian	21	"	"	"
Duncan McIntyre	47	"	Farmer	Over Rented.
Helen McNab	42	"	Wife	"
Alexr. McIntyre	20	"	Farmer	"
Duncan McIntyre	15	"	Child	"
John McIntyre	13	"	"	"
Margt. McIntyre	10	"	"	"
Donald McNaughton	19	"	Farmer	"
Peter McCullum	27	"	"	"
George Thomson	41	"	"	"
Janet Wilson	40	"	Wife	"
Peter Thomson	18	"	Farmer	"
Hugh McGrigor	42	"	"	"
Jean McNaughton	38	"	Wife	"
Donald McGrigor	14	"	Child	"
Kathn. McGrigor	12	"	"	"
Angus McNaughton	29	"	Farmer	"
Kathn. Robertson	24	"	Wife	"
John McNaughton	6	"	Child	"
Jean McNaughton	4	"	"	"
Duncan McMartine	63	"	Farmer	"
Isobell McGrigor	59	"	Wife	"
Margt. McMartine	24	"	Servant	Want of business.
Hugh McMartine	21	"	"	"
Donald McMartine	20	"	Wright	"

(P.R.O.) (T. 47/12)

PORT GREENOCK.

List of Passengers from this Port from 7th:

July 1775. Inclusive to the 14th: July Exclusive.

Names.	Age.	Occupations.	Former Residence.	On what account & for what purpose they go.	In what Ship they take their Passage.
James Irvine	22	Planter	Dumfries	To follow his) Employment.)	
Lauchlan Fraser	17	as a Planter	Inverness	do.	
David Alexander	19	Merchant	Maybole	do.	
William Stewart	25	do.	Air	do.	
Nathl. Anderson	17	Clerk	Alloa	do.	
Alexander Dallas	18	Merchant	Aberdeen	do.	
Peter Campbell	20	do.	Glasgow	do.	
George McKay	16	Farmer	Sutherland	To be a Planter	
David Turnbull	18	Land-) survayor)	Glasgow	To follow his) Employment.)	
James McLean	16	Merchant	Air	do.	
John Nisbet	18	Wright	Glasgow	do.	
George Robertson	34	Merchant	Aberdeen	To a Friend.	
John Horn	23	Black-) smith)	Banff	To follow his) Employment.)	Pr. the
John Mills	24	Merchant	Aberdeen	do.	Isobella
James Jack	18	do.	do.	To a Friend.	William
Doctor Gilpen	30	Surgeon	Whitehaven	To live upon) his property.)	McLenan Master for
David Easter	19	Merchant	Shire of Ross	To follow his) Employment.)	Jamaica.
Walter Collan	20	do.	Edinburgh	To follow his) business.)	
Mrs. Ross & Daughter			do.	To her Husband.	
George Little	19	Merchant	Dumfries	To follow his) Employment.)	
William Creighton	18	do.	Edinburgh	do.	
John Smith	19	do.	Down	do.	
James Mitchell	20	do.	do.	do.	
Danl. Ferguson	17	Taylor	do.	do.	
James Gilmor	23	Mill Wright	Ireland	do.	
John Middleton	19	Clerk	Stonehaven	do.	

Total 27.   (Signed)

(EDWARD PENMAN D. Collr.
(JOHN McVICAR D. Compr,
(JOHN DUNLOP Tidesurver.

(P.T.O.)

(P.R.O.) (T. 47/12)

Port Stornoway.

An account of the Number of Persons who have

Emigrated to America in the Ship "Clementina" of Philadelphia,

Patrick Brown Master.

Persons Names.	Ages.	Quality	Occupation or Employment.	Former Residence.	Parts or places to which they have gone.	On what account and for what purpose they have left the country.
Duncan Sinclair	10	Servant		Inverness	Philadelphia	
John Sinclair	15	"		"	"	
Jannet McPherson	18	"		"	"	
John Fennister	10	"		Avis	"	
Jean Grant	19	"		Builie	"	
Margaret McQueen	16	"		Braen	"	
Isobell McQueen	10	"		"	"	
Duncan McQueen	14	"		"	"	
Anne Munro	18	"		Balconie	"	
Anne Kelly	15	"		Contin	"	
Dond. Tolmie	18	"		Downie Castle	"	
Isobell Astine	18	"	Served in	Nairn	"	All Emigrants
Anne Taylor	19	"	different	Findorn	"	in hope of
John Rabb	27	"	kinds of	Duffus	"	procuring a
Thomas McKenzie	18	"	services.	Fairburn	"	better live-
Alexr. McKenzie	20	"		"	"	lihood.
Alexr. McDond.	21	"		Strathpaifer	"	
John Shaw	14	"		Fordardich	"	
John Sutherland	22	"		Duffus	"	
Murdock McLeanan	10	"		Builie	"	
Dond. McPhail	9	"		Leys	"	
John Kennedy	17	"		"	"	
Dond. McCra	9	"		Kinmily	"	
Murdock McLeod	18	"		Contin	"	
Rory Provest	18	"		Belmaduthy	"	
Paul Provest	15	"		"	"	
Betty Rose	17	"		Inverness	"	
Jannet Fraser	18	"		"	"	
Christian McDond.	18	"		Builie	"	
David Stivins	19	"		Inverness	"	
John McLeanan	32	"		Isle of Sky	"	
Isobell McPherson	21	"		Inverness	"	
John McKenzie	18	"		"	"	
Catherine McDond.	18	"		"	"	

(Preceding Account Continued.)

Alexr. McDond.	24	Servant	Duffus	Philadelphia	
Will. Anderson	23	"	Anass	"	
Will. McKay	24	"	Duffus	"	
James Watson	25	"	"	"	
Anne McQuire	12	"	Braen	"	
Alexr. McCullock	25	"	"	"	
Christian McKenzie	12	"	Wester leys	"	
Marjory McKenzie	20	"	"	"	
John McKenzie	11	"	Builie	"	
John McKenzie	14	"	Wester leys	"	
Mary Morison	22	"	Inverness	"	
Malcolm McLeod	15	"	Contin	"	
Jannet McPherson	12	"	Inverness	"	
Isobell McKenzie	13	"	Wester leys	"	
John McPherson	21	"	Inverness	"	
James McDond.	10	"	Builie	"	
Archbd. McDond.	18	"	"	"	
Janet McDond.	18	"	"	"	
Geo. Morison	15	"	"	"	
John Morison	17	"	"	"	
Hugh Morison	13	"	"	"	
Bathia McDonald	15	"	"	"	
Dond. McKenzie	13	"	Wester Leys	"	
Will McPhail	17	"	Served in	"	"	All emigrated
Alexr. Shaw	20	"	different	Daimie	"	in the hope
Mary McDonald	18	"	kinds of	Builie	"	of procuring
Jannet Cameron	18	"	Services.	Lochbroom	"	a better
John McPhail	36	"		Wester Leys	"	livelihood.
Margaret McKenzie	22	"		Inverness	"	
Margaret Munro	21	"		"	"	
Margaret McPherson	21	"		"	"	
Margaret McKenzie	23	"		Culduthel	"	
Isobell Jack	14	"		Kilsain	"	
Donald Cameron	24	"		Ft. Augustus	"	
Isobell McDonald	15	"		Inverness	"	
Murdock McKenzie	37	"		Wester leys	"	
Jean McPherson	20	"		"	"	
John Mitchell	24	"		Rothy May	"	
Isobell Fraser	17	"		Builie	"	
Mary Fraser	17	"		"	"	
Isobell Fraser	21	"		"	"	
Anne McCra	23	"		Inverness	"	
Will. Kennedy	36	"		Wester leys	"	
Hugh McCra	11	"		Kinmily	"	
Mary McDonald	30	"		"	"	
Elizabeth McKenzie	12	"		Wester leys	"	
Andrew Urchart	20	"		Duffus	"	
Mary Fraser	18	"		Park	"	
John Urchart	30	"		Duffus	"	
Donald Forbes	39	"		Inverness	"	
Alexr. McIntosh	21	"		Bailnacoter	"	

(Preceding Account Continued.)

Name	Age	Status	Remarks	Origin	Destination	Note
Anne Bailly	25	Servant		Inverness	Philadelphia	
Elspia McDond.	16	"		Kinmily	"	
Anne McLeanan	13	"		Builie	"	
Kenneth McKenzie	14	"		"	"	
Elspi° Campbell	30	"		"	"	
John McPhail	15	"		Wester leys	"	
Alexr. McPhail	12	"		"	"	
Alexr. McLeanan	40	"		Builie	"	
John McKay	16	"		"	"	
Mary Kennedy	10	"		Wester leys	"	
Anne Kennedy	11	"		"	"	
Will. McDonald	16	"		Builie	"	
Donald Kennedy	20	"		Wester leys	"	
Alexr. Kennedy	13	"		"	"	
Will. Kennedy	13	"		"	"	
John Clerk	37	"		Findorn	"	
Jannet Forbes	18	"	Served in	Inverness	"	
Donald Fraser	15	"	different	Dunbalich	"	
Isobell McKenzie	28	"	kinds of	Braen	"	
Alexr. Fimister	16	"	Services.	Murray	"	
James Hendry	20	"		"	"	
Will. Kemp	18	"		"	"	
Elspia Fimister	14	"		"	"	
Margaret Fimister	12	"		"	"	
Jannet Jack	23	"		"	"	All emigrated
Thomas McKenzie	22	"		Builie	"	in hope of
John Jack	30	"		Murray	"	procuring a
Alexr. Laing	21	"		"	"	better live-
Alexr. Brown	12	"		Wester leys	"	lihood.
Mary Montgomery	19	"		Inverness	"	
Anne McLeanan	20	"		Ferintosh	"	
Maron McLeanan	18	"		Inverness	"	
John Thomson	33	"		Burghead	"	
John Menzies	21	"		Inverness	"	
Alexr. Robinson	20	Passenger.	Just from his educa-tion.)	Lochbroom	"	
James Chissim	42	"	Farmer	Builie	"	
Mathia McDonald	18	Servant		"	"	
Hugh McDonald	25	"		Lochbroom	"	
Elizabeth McDonald	21	"		"	"	
Donald Cameron	65	Passenger	Farmer	Builie	"	
John Cameron	34	"	"	"	"	
Simon Cameron	29	"	"	"	"	
Jean Fraser	25	"		"	"	
Anne McKenzie	25	"		"	"	
Charles Cameron	5	"		"	"	
Mary Cameron	3	"		"	"	
Catherine Cameron	½	"		"	"	
Catherine McKenzie	29	"		"	"	

84

(Preceding Account Continued.)

Name	Age				
Donald McDonald	58	Passenger	Labourer	Kinmily	Philadelphia
Hugh Brown	38	"	Farmer	Inverness	"
Margory Brown	30	" Wife		"	"
Andrew McIntosh	27	Passenger	Labourer	Elgin	"
George Russell	18	"	Farmer	Avis	"
Alexr. McPherson	58	"	"	Inverness	"
John Provest	43	Passenger	Farmer	Siddy	"
Isobell Provost	30	"	" Wife	"	"
John Provest	3	"	" Son	"	"
Alexr. Provest	2	"	" Son	"	"
Will Fraser	26	"	Wright	Inverness	"
Anne Fraser	26	"	" Wife	"	"
John Fraser	40	"	Farmer	Kinmily	"
Christian Fraser	31	"	" Wife	"	"
Jannet Fraser	9	"	" daughter	"	"
Margaret Fraser	6	"	" "	"	"
Will. Fraser	3	"	" Son	"	"
Jean Fraser	1	"	" daughter	"	"
John Clerk	29	"	Farmer	Inverness	"
Betty Clerk	29	"	" Wife	"	"
Margaret Clerk	1	"	" daughter	"	"
Peter Morison	47	"	Fisher	Builie	"
Anne Morison	44	"	" Wife		
Betty Morison	14	"	" daughter		"
Catherine Morison	2½	"	" "	"	"
James McKairick	35	"	Farmer	Murray	"
Mary McKairick	32	"	" Wife	"	"
John McKairick	12	"	" Son	"	"
Alexr. McKairick	6	"	" "	"	"
Will. McKairick	4	"	" "	"	"
Elizabeth McKairick	½	"	" daughter	"	"
Kenneth McKenzie	38	"	Farmer	Fairburn	"
John McKenzie	14	"	" Son	"	"
Mary McKenzie	16	"	" daughter	"	"
Kenneth McFwer	24	"	Labourer	Lochbroom	"
Alexr. McKay	27	"	"	Builie	"
Anne McKay	29	"	" Wife	"	"
Jean McKay	1½	"	" daughter	"	"
John Sinclair	45	"	Taylor	Inverness	"
Duncan McDonald	50	"	Farmer	Builie	"
Christian McDonald	40	"	" Wife	"	"
Will. Fimister	46	"	Farmer	Avis	"
Elizabeth Femister	50	"	" Wife	"	"
Alexr. McKenzie	42	"	Weaver	Inverness	"
Isobell McKenzie	40	"	" Wife	"	"
Anne McKenzie	8	"	" daughter	"	"
Catherine McKenzie	5	"	" "	"	"
Isobell McKenzie	½	"	" "	"	"
Alexr. McKenzie	2	"	" Son	"	"
John Watson	22	"	Smith	Duffus	"
Alexr. Dugall	22	"	Farmer	"	"
Archd. Forseyth	22	"	"	"	"

All emigrated
for the Pre-
ceding Reason.

(Preceding Account Continued.)

Name	Age		Occupation	From	Destination	
Alexr. Henderson	24	Passenger	Taylor	Murray	Philadelphia	
John Morison	26	"	Jeaver	Builie	"	
Isobell Fraser(sic)	28	"	" Wife	"	"	
Alexr. Morison	3	"	" Son	"	"	
Isobell McKenzie	40	"		Inverness	"	
Anne McKenzie	3	"		"	"	
John McKenzie	1	"		"	"	
John McKenzie	39	"	Labourer	Builie	"	
Anne McKenzie	39	"	" Wife	"	"	
James McKenzie	5	"	" Son	"	"	
Dond. McKenzie	2	"	" "	"	"	
Jean McPhail	86	"		Inverness	"	All
Duncan McPhail	3	"		"	"	emigrated
Jean McPhail	½	"		"	"	for the
Anne Kennedy	40	"		Wester leys	"	Preceding
Margaret Kennedy	1	"		"	"	Reason.
Isobell Thomson	40	"		Burghead	"	
John Thomson	9	"		"	"	
Isobell Thomson	7	"		"	"	
Will. Thomson	5	"		"	"	
Geo. Thomson	2	"		"	"	
Margaret Clerk	32	"		Findorn	"	
Margaret Clerk	9	"		"	"	
John Clerk	6	"		"	"	
Janet Clerk	4	"		"	"	
Jean Clerk	1½	"		"	"	
Will. Mitchell	33	"		Fife	"	

No. of Men Emigrated = 90

" " Women " = 68

" " Children " = 54

Customho. Stornoway 13th of July 1775.

ARCHD SMITH Collr.
JOHN REID Compr.

(Endorsed)   Port Storny.
List of Emigrants
Shipped on board
the "Clementina"of
and for Philadelphia.
Pat. Brown, Mar.

Port Greenock.

List of Passengers from this Port from 14th: July

1775, Inclusive to the 21st: of July 1775, Exclusive.

Names.	Former Residence.	Occupation & Employment.	Age.	To what Port or Place Bound.	On what Account & for what purpose they go.	In what ship they take their Passage.
David Campbell	Edinburgh	Writer	40	Georgia	To follow his business.	In the
Mrs. Campbell	do.		40	in	following her husband.	Georgia
David Campbell)			6	North	)	Thomas
Ann Campbell)		Their	8	America.	)following their	Boltan
Jean Campbell)	do.	Children	1		)Parents.	for
Mary Campbell)			3		)	Georgia
Susie Campbell)			4		)	
Betty Campbell)			5		)	
Walter Spence	do.	Merchant	25		To follow his business.	
Thomas Peton	Glasgow	(An Officer (in the Army.	25		To Join the Regiment.	
Jno. McKinnon	Mull	Farmer	28		Too High Rented.	
Archd. McKinnon	do.	do.	40		do.	
Janet his Spouse	do.		30		Following her Husband.	
Thomas Gillespie	Downe	do.	20		Too High Rented.	
John Ferguson	do.	do.	25		do.	
Janet his Spouse			20		Following her Husband.	
John Gillespie	do.	do.	25		Too High Rented.	
Archd. McLochlan	do.	do.	29		do.	
William Gordon	Aberdeen	Merchant	25		To follow his business.	
Rosl. McFarlane	Kippen	Wright	28		do.	
Janet his Spouse	do.				To follow her Husband.	
Stair Lighton	Edinburgh	Clerk	28		Want of Employment.	
Walter Stewart	do.	Wright	25		do.	
Archd. Lundie	do.	Merchant	25		To follow his Business.	

Total 24.　　　　　　　(SIGNED)　　(EDWARD PERMAN D. Collr.
　　　　　　　　　　　　　　　　　(JOHN McVICAR D. Comptr.
　　　　　　　　　　　　　　　　　(JOHN DUNLOP.

(P.R.O.) (T. 47/12

Port Greenock.

List of Passengers from the 28th July

1775 Inclusive to 4th August 1775 Exclusive.

Names	Former Residence.	Age.	Occupation.	To what Place.	On what Account.	
Walter Colhoun	Glasgow	30	Merchant	Antigua	(To follow his (Business.	)p. the)Chance
Francis Stewart	do.	25	A Gentleman	do.	For his health.	)John
Willm. Scoure	Stirling	22	A Merchant	do.	(To follow his (Business.	)McWhae)for
Thomas Frazer	Air	21	(A custom ho. (Clerk	do	(To be a (Merchant.	)Antegua.)
Willm. Hume	Glasgow	40	Ship Master	Georgia	To Recover Debts.	)
Robt. Park	Greenock	24	Clerk	do.	Storekeeper.	)p. the
John Coupar	Lochinock	16	do.	do.	do.	)Christy
Daniel Baine	Greenock	30	Mariner	do.	for a New Ship.	)Andrew
James Scott	do.	33	do.	do.	do.	)Lee
Daniel Clerk	do.	32	Carpenter	do.	do.	)Master
James Logan	do.	30	Sail Maker	do.	do.	)for
Andew. McFadine	do.	36	Joiner	do.	For Employment.	)Georgia
Jas. McFadine	do.	17	do.	do.	do.	)

ED. PENMAN D. Collr.
JCHN McVICAR D. Compr.
JCHN DUNLOP.

13.

(Endorsed)

Port Greenock
List of Passengers
from 26th July 1775 Inclusive
to the 4th August 1775 Exclusive.

(P.R.O.) (T. 47/12)

A List of Passengers or Emigrants on Board the Ship
"Jupiter"of Larne Samuel Brown Master for Wilmington in North
Carolina their Names, Ages, Occupations or Employments and
Former Residence.

No.	Names.	Ages.	Occupation or Employment.	Former Residence.
1	John Stewart	48	Clothier	Glenurchy.
2	Elizabeth	46	His Wife	do.
3	John Stewart	15	their Son	do.
4	Margaret	13	their Daughter	do.
5	Janet	12	do.	do.
6	Patrick Stewart	6	their Son	do.
7	Elizabeth	3	their Daughter	do.
8	Donald MacIntire	54	Labourer	do.
9	Katherine	41	His Wife	do.
10	Mary	12	their daughter	do.
11	Margaret	9	do.	do.
12	John McIntire	6	their Son	do.
13	Duncan McIntire	5	do.	do.
14	William Campbell	28	Labourer	do.
15	Katherine	32	His Wife	do.
16	Robert Campbell	2	His Son	do.
17	Duncan Campbell		do. an Infant	do.
18	Donald MacNichol	40	Labourer	do.
19	Katherine	33	His Wife	do.
20	John McNicol	6½	their Son	do.
21	Nicol McNicol	4	do.	do.
22	Archibald McNicol	2	do.	do.
23	Mary		their daughter an Infant	do.
24	John McIntire	35	Labourer	do.
25	Ann	32	His Wife	do.
26	Margaret	6	their Daughter	do.
27	Archibald McIntire	4	their Son	do.
28	John McIntire		do. an Infant	do.
29	Archibald Stewart	30	Shoemaker	do.
30	Ann Sinclair	65	Spinster	do.
31	Margaret her Daughter	25	do.	do.
32	Ann McIntire	60	do.	do.
33	Christian Downy	25	do.	do.
34	Katherine McVane	30	Spinster	do.
35	Mary Downie	4	her Daughter	do.
36	Joseph Downie an Infant		her Son	do.

37	Dugal McCole	38	Labourer	do.
38	Ann	38	His Wife	do.
39	Marget	10	their Daughter	do.
40	Mary	8	do.	do.
41	Sarah	2	do.	do.
42	An Infant		do.	do.
43	Angus McNicol	30	Labourer	do.
44	Ann	20	His Wife	do.
45	Dougald Stewart	40	Labourer	do.
46	His Wife	40	do.	do.
47	John Stewart	16	their Son	do.
48	James Stewart	10	do.	do.
49	Thomas Stewart	6	do.	do.
50	Alexander Stewart	4	do.	do.
51	Allan Stewart	44	Late Lieut. in Frasers) Regiment.)	Alpine.
52	Donald Carmichael	22	His servant	do
53	Lilly Stewart	7	his natural daughter	do.
54	Alexander Stewart	35	Gentleman Farmer	do.
55	Charles Stewart	15	His Son	do.
56	John McCole	49	Labourer	do.
57	Milrid McCole	40	His Wife	do.
58	John McCole	16	their Son	do.
59	Samuel McCole	15	their Son	do.
60	Donald McCole	12	do.	do.
61	Dougald McCole	8	do.	do.
62	Alexander McCole	4	do.	do.
63	Katherine	2	their Daughter	do.
64	Evan Carmichael	40	Labourer	do.
65	Margaret	38	His Wife	do.
66	Archibald Carmichael	14	their Son	do.
67	Allan Carmichael	12	do.	do.
68	Katherine	2	their Daughter	do.
69	Duncan McCole	35	Farmer	do.
70	Christian	35	His Wife	do.
71	Dugald McCole	20	their Son	do.
72	Christian	2	their Daughter	do.
73	Katherine	3	do.	do.
74	Malcolm McInish	40	Labourer	do.
75	Jannet	36	His Wife	do.
76	John McInish	20	their Son	do.
77	Ann	15	their Daughter	do.
78	Catherine	11	do.	do.
79	Donald McInish	8	their Son	do.
80	Archibald McInish	4	do.	do.
81	Kenneth Stewart	40	late Ship Master	do.
82	Isobel	30	His Wife	do.
83	Alexander Stewart	14	their Son	do.
84	John Stewart	5	do.	do.
85	Banco Stewart	3	do.	do.
86	Christian	3	their Daughter	do.
87	William an Infant	"	their Son	do.
88	Mary Black	16	their Servant	do.
89	Christian Carmichael	14	do.	do.

90	John Black	14	do.	do.
91	Dugald Carmichael	55	Farmer	do.
92	Mary	55	His Wife	do.
93	Archibald Colquhown	22	her Son	do.
94	Ann Colquhown	20	her Daughter	do.
95	Donald McCole	34	Labourer	do.
96	Katherine	40	His Wife	do.
97	Evan McCole	6	their Son	do.
98	John McIntyre	32	Taylor	do.
99	Katherine	30	his Wife	do.
100	Donald McIntyre	3	their Son	do.
101	John McIntyre	1	do.	do.
102	Gilbert McIntyre	34	Taylor	do.
103	Ann	36	his Wife	do.
104	Charles McIntyre	11	their Son	do.
105	Margaret	9	their Daughter	do.
106	Evan McIntyre	5	their Son	do.
107	Malcolm McIntyre	1	do.	do.
108	Duncan McCole	45	Farmer	do.
109	Christian	40	His Wife	do.
110	Duncan McCole	21	His Son	do.
111	Mary	18	their Daughter	do.
112	Sarah	15	do.	do.
113	Christian	10	do.	do.
114	Milrid	6	do.	do.
115	Ann	3	do.	do.
116	Donald Black	45	Labourer	Lismore
117	Jannet	34	His Wife	do.
118	Christian	8	his Daughter	do.
119	Ann	4	do.	do.
120	Ewen	4	their Son	do.
121	Duncan	1½	do.	do.
122	Archibald Carmichael	26	Labourer	do.
123	Mary	26	His Wife	do.
124	Catherine	17	their Daughter	do.
125	Lachlan McLaren	25	Labourer	Alpine
126	Lawrine McLaren	20	Joiner	do.
127	Donald McLaren	12	Labourer	do.
128	Duncan McLaren	30	do.	do.
129	David McCole	30	do.	do.
130	Duncan McIntyre	55	do.	do.
131	Katherine	55	His Wife	do.
132	May	24	their Daughter	do.
133	Katherine	17	do.	do.
134	Elizabeth	14	do.	do.
135	Miss Christy McDonald	25	Seamstress	do.
136	Duncan McCallum	30	Labourer	do.

Reasons assigned by the Persons named on this and ye

three preceding Pages of this List for their Emigrating

follows Viz[t]: The Farmers and Labourers who are taking
their Passage in this Ship unanimously declare that they
never would have thought of leaving their native Country,
could they have supplied their Families in it. But such
of them as were Farmers were obliged to quit their Lands
either on account of the advanced Rent or to make room
for Shepherds. Those in particular from Alpine say that
out of one hundred Mark Land that formerly was occupied
by Tennants who made their Rents by rearing Cattle and
raising Grain, Thirty three Mark Land of it is now turned
into Sheep Walks and they seem to think in a few years
more, Two thirds of that Country, at least will be in the
same State so of course the greatest part of the Inhabitants
will be obliged to leave it. The Labourers Declare they
could not support their families on the Wages they earned
and that it is not from any other motive but the dread of
want & that they quit a Country which above all others
they would wish to live in. Captain Allan Stewart formerly
a Lieutenant in Fraser's Regiment goes with an Intention
of Settling in the Lands granted him by the Government
at the End of last War. But should the Troubles continue
in America he is Determined to make the Best of his way
to Boston and Offer his Service to General Gage.

The Tradesmen have a prospect of getting better
Wages but their principal reason seems to be that their

relations are going and rather than part with them they choose to go along.

(Signed)   (DUNCAN CAMPBELL Collector.
              (NEIL CAMPBELL Comptroller.

September 4th: 1775.

(P.R.O.) (T. 47/12)

Port Kirkwall.   An Account of People going from Orkney and Caithness in the "Marlborough"

Thomas Walker Master for Savannah in Georgia as indented Servants to

Messrs. Jonas Brown & Company of Whitby.

No.	Names	Ages.	Quality.	Employment.	Former Residence.	Reasons for Emigrating.
1	William Miller	39	Married	Farmer	Evie in Orkney	His far so high rented) that he could not live) by it.)
2	Margaret Irvine his Wife	36	Do.	lived with) her Parents))	Do.	Goes with her husband.
3	Isobel Miller	16	Unmarried			
4	Hugh Miller	14	Do.	Do.		Go with their Parents.
5	William Miller	11	Do.	Do.		
6	John Miller	5	Do.	Do.		
7	James Robertson	36	Married	Servant to a) Farmer.	Do.	To try to better his) fortune.
8	Christian Linay his Wife	26	Do.		Do.	Goes with her husband.
9	William Bews	39	Do.	Farmer	Do.	His farm too high rented.
10	Christian Smith his Wife	30	Do.		Do.	Goes with her husband.
11	Nicol Johnston	28	Do.	Farmer	Do.	Could not live by his) farm.
12	Isobel Flett his Wife	28	Do.		Do.	Goes with her husband.
13	Jannet Johnston an Infant					
14	Robert Garson	50	Do.	Servant to a) farmer.	Sandwick in) Orkney)	Could not get Employment. N.B. This man has a very bad) character.
15	Alex. Calder	42	Do.	Wright	Wick in Caithness	Could not support his) family by his business) at home.
16	Henrietta Bain his Wife	32	Do.		Do.	Goes with her husband.

No.	Name	Age		Occupation	Place	Remarks
17	Katherine Calder	16)				
18	Robert Calder	14)		lived with their Parents)	Do.	Go with their Parents.
19	John Calder	12)				
20	James Calder	8)				
21	Christian Calder	6)				
22	Peggy Calder	2)				
23	William Manson	24	Married	Weaver	Dunnet in Caithness)	Could not live so well at home as he thought he could do abroad.
24	Elizabeth Sinclair his) Wife.)	24	Do.		Do.	Goes with her husband.
25	James Brock	21	a Porter		Kirkwall in Orkney.)	To try to better his fortune.
26	James Corrigil	22	Do.	Servant to a Farmer.)	Wick in Caithness	The same reason.
27	Francis Sutherland	19	Do.	Weaver	Do.	Ditto.
28	George McBeath	19	Do.	Servant to a Farmer.)	Do.	Ditto.
29	Alexander Grant	20	Do.	a Piper	Latieron in Do.	Ditto.
30	William Whair	20	Do.	Servant to a Farmer.)	Wick in Do.	Ditto.
31	William Bain	26	Do.	Weaver	Do.	Could not live by his Trade.
32	James Sinclair	20	Do.	Servant to a Farmer.)	Holm in Orkney	Hard labour and small Wages.
33	David Murray	20	Do.	House Carpenter	Kirkwall in Do.	To try to better his fortune.
34	Alexander Moar	18	Do.	Ditto.	Ditto.	Ditto.
35	Michael Robertson	20	Do.	Servant to a Farmer.)	Harray in Do.	Ditto.
36	William Bremner	21	Do.	House Carpenter	Kirkwall	Ditto.
37	George Bunson	18	Do.	Shoemaker	Do.	Ditto.
38	James Irvine	17	Do.	Servant to a Farmer.)	Evie in Do.	Ditto.
39	Murdoch Mackay	20	Do.	a Piper	Bowar in Caithness	Ditto.
40	William Sutherland	15	Do.	Servant to his Father.)	Dunnet in Do.	Used ill by his Parents.

No.	Name	Age		Occupation	Residence	Reason
41	Jannet Horn	22	Do.	a Servant	Wick in Do.	To try to better his fortune.)
42	Anne Leal	21	Do.	Ditto.	Canisbay in Do.	Used ill by her Master.
43	Janet Reech	20	Do.	Ditto.	Wick in Do.	To try to better her fortune.)
44	Elizabeth Miller	28	Do.	Ditto.	Bowar in Do.	Ditto.
45	David Tait her Son	7	Do.		Do.	Goes with his Mother.
46	Margaret Sinclair	20	Do.	Ditto.	Do.	To try to better her fortune.)
47	Elizabeth Corrigtl	20	Do.	Ditto.	Kirkwall in Orkney	Ditto.
48	Jannet Johnston	21	Do.	Ditto.	Ewie in Do.	Ditto.
49	Jannet Traill	23	Do.	Ditto.	Kirkwall	Ditto.
50	Jannet Alexander	23	Do.	Ditto.	Eaglesbay in Do.	Ditto.
51	Jannet Manson	19	Do.	Ditto.	Dunnet in Caithness	Ditto.
52	John Korn	12	Do.	Ditto.	Birsay in Orkney	Ditto.
53	Hugh Isbister	20	Do.	a Boatman	Stromess in "	Ditto.

(Accompanying letter endorsed.)

Sept. 25th 1775.
Commrs. Customs
in Scotland.
Wh. List of Emigrants.

(P.R.O.) (T. 47/12)

List of Emigrants on Board the "Lovely Nelly" Wm. Sheridan

Master Bound for St. Johns Island in North America Viz.

Persons Names	Trade.	Age.	Place or Residence.	Parish.	Reasons for leaving the Country.
John Smith	Black) smith)	33) Years) old)	Lachend	Colvend	Could not earn Bread.) Sufficient to support) him & his family.)
Margt. McViccar		28	Do.		
Wm. & Mary Smith		6 & 5			
John McGeorge		24			
Jean Stevenson		66			
James Wardrop	Mason	26	Haliaths	Lochmaben	Same Reason.
David Harrieson	Wheel-) wright)	40	Eulifechan	Haddon	Same Reason.
Jannet Henderson		44			
Grizell Harrieson		19			
Agness Do.		17			
Helen Do.		13			
Jannet & Margt. Do.		9 & 7			
John Crocket	Farmer	31	Thornyhill	Colvend	Same Reason.
Margt. Young		28			
Jas. Crocket		6			
Wm. & Jas. Crockets		4 & 1			
John McCracken		23			
Walwood Waugh	Joiner	33	Brownmoor	Annan	Same Reason.
Helen Henderson		30			
Four Boys & one) Girl. . . . . .)		from 10 to 1			
Cathn. Colven		30			
Margt. Campbell		26			
Wm. Campbell		24			
Wm. McKie	Mason	30	Cassaend	Kelton	Same Reason.
Issabell McKie		29			
John Eliza. & Mary McKie		6, 4 & 1			
Wm. Troop	Mason	24	Do.	Do.	Same Reason.
John Troop	Labourer	22			
Alexr. Coupland	Do.	18			
Wm. McBurnie	Joiner	26	Fairgirth	Colvend	Same Reason.
Ro. McBurnie	Do.	20			
Barbra Henning					
Thos. Wm. & Christn.) Armstrongs)	Labour-) ers.)	(17,15 (& 10	Nether-) miln.)	Glencairn	Same Reason.
Chas. Blackie	Farmer	36	Milnbank	Suthwick	Could not with all) his Industry support) himself & family.)
Jannet Herries		36			

John Blackie		6			
Wm. Do.		4			
James Do.		8			
Ann Do.		10 Mos.			
James Taylor	Wright	25			
Ro. Blair	Sailor	50	Drum	Newabby	Same Reason.
Henny Shannen		20			
John Smith	Mason	45	Preston	Kirkbean	Same Roason.
Jant. Sturgeon					
Jant. Smith		6			
Mary Do.		16			
Jan Do.		9			
Agness Do.		5			
Issabela Do.		3:			
Nelly Do.		1			
Ro Coultart	Labourer	20	Lashmack-) wharren.)	Kirkgunzeon	Same Reason.
Wm. Smith	Do.	24	Corsack	Colvend	Same Reason.
Mary Wilson		50			
Ro. Stewart	Do.	16	Knockhuley	Suthwick	Same Reason.
Jannet Stewart		14			
Wm. Wilson	Labourer	23	Boreland	Colvend	Same Reason.
John Wilson	Do.	21	Do.	Do.	Same Reason.

(Undated)

INDEX OF PERSONS.

110

112

116